LIVING MOUNTAINS

How and Why Volcanoes Erupt

JACQUES KORNPROBST AND CHRISTINE LAVERNE

2006
Mountain Press Publishing Company
Missoula, Montana

This book was translated from the original work *Les Volcans: comment ça marche*, which was first published in France in 2002 in the series *Geosciences* by *Editions Scientifiques GB* in collaboration with the Société Géologique de France and the Éditions du BRGM.

Library of Congress Cataloging-in-Publication Data

Kornprobst, Jacques.
   Living mountains : how and why volcanoes erupt / Jacques Kornprobst and Christine Laverne.
     p. cm.
Includes index.
ISBN-13: 978-0-87842-513-6 (pbk. : alk. paper)
   1. Volcanoes—Popular works. 2. Volcanic eruptions—Popular works.
I. Laverne, Christine. II. Title.
QE522.K67 2006
551.21—dc22
                                        2005025736

PRINTED IN HONG KONG BY MANTEC PRODUCTION COMPANY

Mountain Press Publishing Company
P.O. Box 2399 • Missoula, Montana
406-728-1900

CONTENTS

FOREWORD

The first aim of scientific research is to explain natural phenomena. Some of these phenomena conveniently present themselves as clear consequences of the simple laws governing the universe: the apple that fell in front of Newton's eyes or the moon orbiting the earth for all mankind to see are events easily explained by the law of gravity. The variables, in these cases, are few and well defined: mass and distance.

A volcanic eruption, though—how does that work? A volcano is a good example of a mechanism with many variables falling into several categories: mechanical, physical, and chemical. Depending on the diversity of circumstances, there is a corresponding variety of resulting events. The art of the volcanologist consists of establishing plausible relationships between causes (which he or she needs to know how to quantify) and effects (which he or she is supposed to observe faithfully).

To understand the causes of a volcanic eruption is the equivalent of having precise and absolute knowledge of the makeup and physical properties of the earth, from the surface down to its center. To understand the effects requires an ability to measure all the variables that could be significant in relation to the volcanic activity on our planet. The relationships between causes and effects, once they are well established, are also useful in the opposite sense: volcanoes have taught us a lot about the depths of the earth.

Volcanology, a scientific discipline with a long history, is also a good example of the way in which research today has become fundamentally multidisciplinary. All areas concerning solid matter, liquids and gases, crystallography, mechanics, the physics of fluids and solids, and thermodynamics play their part as volcanologists try to unravel the mysteries of volcanoes. Volcanologists also integrate information technology in their study; computer modeling plays an essential role in the study of complex phenomena. Even nuclear physics plays a role: dating methods that geologists employ are based on this science.

Therefore, to be interested in volcanoes is to be interested in science as a whole. In reading this book you will explore diverse fields of knowledge. Besides the pleasure of understanding, will this book give you a certain confidence in the future? Can the hiccups and burps of the earth be precisely predicted in order to protect us more effectively? The authors describe recent progress in the methods of volcanic surveillance and prediction. We see promise and limitations in these methods. We listen in on our planet thanks to a large number of lasers, radars, sound waves, and satellites. We learn more how to interpret what we hear and see. Is that to say, then, that very soon we will be able to keep volcanoes quiet? Unfortunately, no, but at least we will know what to do in response to volcanic events.

HUBERT CURIEN
Former President of the French Academy of Sciences
Former Minister for Research in France

PREFACE

A volcano is one of the most beautiful and impressive sights in nature. The pyrotechnics, ear-splitting explosions, and rivers of molten rock are fascinating, and they combine to inspire both fear and admiration.

For a long time people believed volcanoes were outlets of fire from hell. For thousands of years, only the most adventurous would get close to a crater. Prometheus reportedly did so to get fire. Fellow Greek Empedocles and the Roman Pliny the Elder were drawn to the beauty of volcanoes and sought to understand them better. However, apart from posthumous fame, none of them got much reward for their curiosity!

Scientists have studied volcanoes in detail for the last two hundred years, and what we now know is well publicized. Despite this, volcanic activity still retains its mystery for most people, and many misconceptions persist. Yet the mechanisms governing the origin of eruptions and the diversity of volcanic rocks erupted onto the surface of the earth are fairly easy to understand with a bit of concentration. We hope *Living Mountains* will answer most of your questions.

ACKNOWLEDGMENTS

While creating this book, the authors profited from the help and advice of the following people: Pierre Boivin, Yves Caristan, Jean-Jacques Cochemé, Christian Coulon, Hubert Curien, Alain Demant, Bertrand Devouard, Philippe Dupont, François-Dominique de Larouzière, Jean-François Lénat, Martine Métais, Frédéric Nolleau, Françoise Rangin, Pascal Richet, Martine Salvatge, Isabelle Simonnet, Jean-Claude Toutain, Frances Van Wyk De Vries (our translator), Françoise Vidal, Philippe Vidal, and Pierre Vincent. The English version of *Living Mountains* would never have been born had it not been for the friendly help and advice of Dave Vanko. Not only did he introduce us to Mountain Press Publishing, he greatly improved the final French-to-English translation of the book. The final translation from French was also greatly improved by Alan Woodland. James Lainsbury, our editor at Mountain Press, patiently explained English language rules to the authors and, beyond this, was one of the main contributors to the quality of the English translation.

The authors specially thank George Bronner for his artistic advice and for having carried out the digitalization of the watercolors, and also Marie-Claude Kornprobst for her patience and independent advice concerning the text and illustrations. During the long time spent in front of the easel and computer, the authors appreciated the quiet company of their pets Etienne, Anne, Isabelle, Antoine, Félix, Quentin, and Basile.

The authors have drawn information from the work of many others, most notably William C. Albee, Patrick Allard, Patrick Bachélery, Jacques-Marie Bardintzef, Jean-Michel Belin, Pierre Boivin, Jean-Louis Bourdier, Danielle Briot, Robert Brousse, Guy Camus, Jean-Marie Cantagrel, Jean-Louis Cheminée, Vincent Courtillot, Colin H. Donaldson, Timothy Druitt, Jean Fain, Gilbert Féraud, Jean-Baptiste Feriot, Jean Francheteau, Peter Francis, Alain de Goër, Alain Gourgaud, Anita Grunder, C. Guilford, Henri Jaffrezic, Claude Jaupart, Jenda Johnson, Jean-Louis Joron, Thierry Juteau, Katia Krafft, Maurice Krafft, Pierre Lavina, Roger W. Le Maitre, Jean-François Lénat, Alexander McBirney, W. S. MacKenzie, Kristian Magnusson, André Maury, Didier Miallier, Hervé Monestier, James G. Moore, David Needham, Giuseppe Patanè, Claude Rangin, Louis-Philippe Ricard, Claude Robin, Olivier Roche, Stephen Sparks, Thomas Staudacher, Jean-Claude Tanguy, Michel Treuil, Sylvie Vergniolle, Benoit Villemant, and Pierre Vincent.

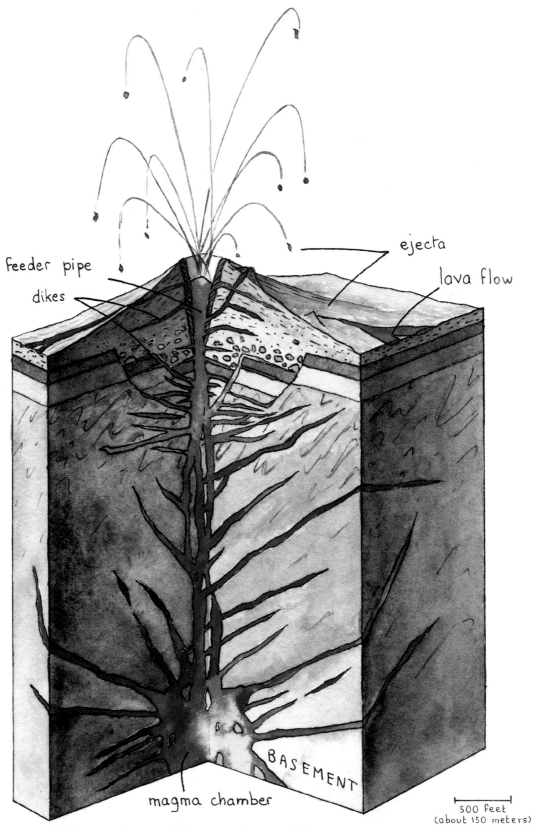

feeder pipe

dikes

ejecta

lava flow

BASEMENT

magma chamber

500 feet
(about 150 meters)

A volcano is fed by a central pipe and dikes.

CONSTRUCTING VOLCANOES

A volcano is the point at which molten rock, which comes from deep within the earth, reaches the earth's surface. It is fed by a central pipe and by dikes that bring molten rock, or magma, to the surface from a magma chamber situated 1,000 feet to 2 miles or more (about 300 meters to over 3 kilometers) beneath the vent. The magma chamber, which is generally very complex in shape, is itself fed by magma from a deeper source, which may be located at depths of up to 200 miles (about 320 kilometers).

In some cases, volcanoes are simply holes in the ground, but generally they form higher relief and are conical in shape. A volcanic cone is built up progressively on a basement of preexisting rock, and it is composed of an accumulation of lavas and volcanic ejecta. The actual shape of a volcano varies depending on the chemical composition and temperature of the erupted lava, as well as the amount of dissolved gas in the magma, which determines the frequency and violence of the eruptions.

SIMPLE AND COMPLEX VOLCANOES

Some volcanoes have a very simple shape because they are built up by just a few eruptions, sometimes by just one eruption. These volcanoes are small cones, or domes, that are built over a few weeks or months. Sunset Crater in Arizona, the small volcanoes of Craters of the Moon National Monument in Idaho, and the Chaîne des Puys volcanic province in the central part of France are all simple volcanoes.

11

At the other extreme, many volcanoes are very complicated, making their structural organization difficult for volcanologists to unravel. These volcanoes tend to be built up from multiple eruptions over long periods of time (thousands, or even hundreds of thousands of years). Phases of lava and pyroclastic accumulation are interspersed with phases of destruction caused by explosive activity, the collapse of a volcano's flanks, or subsidence of basement rock. During these eruptions, and also during the intervals between eruptions, erosion due to runoff shapes the relief of these volcanoes. The volcanoes of the San Francisco Peaks, near Flagstaff, Arizona; the volcanoes of the Cascades in the Pacific Northwest; and the huge Cantal Volcano in central France all belong in this category.

Many volcanoes are very complicated, having developed from multiple eruptions over a long period of time.

LAVAS

Lava plays an important role in the construction of volcanoes, injected as dikes and sills in the basement rock and erupting at the surface as lava flows and domes on the flanks of craters.

Fluid Lavas: Flows and Lava Lakes

Very hot lavas, 2,000 degrees Fahrenheit (about 1,100 degrees Celsius) or more, are fluid and behave almost like water, which is nevertheless much more fluid than any kind of lava! When fluid lava fills a preexisting crater, it constitutes a lava lake. But if a lava lake overflows or if fluid lava emerges directly from a fissure, it can flow rapidly down slopes. Hot lavas build up cones with rather flat profiles, such as Mount Etna in Sicily, or volcanoes with extremely flat profiles, like Mauna Loa on the island of Hawai'i. These lavas run into ravines and valleys where

Hot, fluid lavas can flow rapidly down slopes.

they form long flows that can extend for miles (kilometers to tens of kilometers). Some lavas can flow fairly fast, reaching speeds of 25 to 35 miles per hour (about 40 to 55 kilometers per hour), but generally lava flows do not travel faster than walking pace. They destroy everything in their path but usually are not fatal, since it is easy to avoid them by moving to higher ground.

Pāhoehoe Flows, 'A'a Flows, and Ropy Lavas

On cooling, flows formed from fluid lavas take on various characteristic surface features. The flows may be very smooth and shiny, termed *pāhoehoe*. Or the surface may be rough and composed of disjointed blocks ranging in size from about 1 inch (2 to 3 centimeters) to several feet (1 meter or more); these are called *'a'a* lavas. Both words are derived from the Hawaiian language. 'A'a lavas are rough because gas bubbles are trapped in them as they flow. Pāhoehoe lavas, on the other hand, have completely degassed by the time they flow onto the surface. Pāhoehoe lava has a surface texture of twisted rolls that looks like coils of rope, hence its other name, *ropy lava*. This texture develops when the lava surface in contact with the air, to the depth of a few millimeters, cools and forms a very viscous skin, which refolds on itself while the fluid lava underneath continues flowing. When the folds are less tight, the lava surface is termed *draped*.

Pu'u'O'o, Hawaii

Fluid lavas build up cones with rather flat profiles.

Lava Tunnels

The cooling of a lava flow's surface increases away from a vent until a solid crust forms. It is possible to walk on this crust while the lava continues to flow underneath. Often the roof of a flow will collapse, providing an onlooker with an amazing but dangerous view down into the bubbling lava. Even once the magma supply has lessened, the lava continues to flow downslope due to gravity, leaving behind an intact, hollow tunnel. Occasionally a later flow may travel through the same tunnel, which complicates things when volcanologists try to unravel the history of the volcano that erupted the lava.

Columnar Jointing

As lava cools, it often forms joint-bounded columns with shapes that resemble organ pipes. The columns form once a lava body has solidified and contracted, thus decreasing its total volume, but before the body has cooled completely. At this point the rock is cool enough to fracture, forming regular polygonal jointing along the length of elongated prisms, or *columns*. Usually these columns are hexagonal (six sided) when viewed from above, but they can also be pentagonal or heptagonal (five or seven

Hawaii, 1994

Pāhoehoe lava has a surface texture of twisted rolls that looks like coils of rope, hence its other name, ropy lava.

sided). They form adjacent to, and with their long axes at right angles to, cooling surfaces (the top and bottom of a lava flow). A flow that exhibits columnar jointing is typically characterized by a lower columnar zone, which developed just above the relatively cool ground surface, and an upper columnar zone, which developed downward from the top of the flow's surface. Sandwiched between these two columnar zones, the hardened lava is structurally more chaotic because it continued to slowly move forward in a plastic state as the upper and lower zones solidified.

Columns can also form in dikes and sills. Dikes cut basement rock vertically or obliquely, while sills tend to form roughly horizontal or

The texture of pāhoehoe lava develops when the lava surface cools, forming a very viscous skin that refolds on itself while the fluid lava underneath continues flowing.

It is possible to walk on the solid crust of a cooling lava flow while the lava continues to flow underneath.

parallel to layering within a volcano. The cooling surfaces of dikes are roughly vertical, and consequently the elongated axes of the columns are horizontal. At the margins of a dike, to the thickness of a few millimeters, cooling is almost instantaneous, forming a chilled margin with a very fine grain size; these margins can be glassy. Conversely, the intrusion of hot magma into a dike warms up the surrounding basement rock. If the composition of the basement rock is suitable, it can be "cooked" and transformed into porcellanite, a siliceous rock that resembles unglazed porcelain. The cooling surfaces of sills are horizontal or gently inclined, so the columns that form are vertical; as a result, at first a sill can be confused with a lava flow. Sills, however, have glassy chilled margins—that cooled rapidly—on top and bottom.

Lava lakes form when craters fill with a great quantity of magma. Often the pressure exerted by these lavas causes part of the outer wall of a crater to collapse, initiating a huge lava flow. This happened at Mount Nyiragongo in the Democratic Republic of the Congo (formerly Zaire) in 1977. Lava traveled up to 40 miles per hour (about 65 kilometers per hour) and killed seventy people. However, if the lava remains trapped in the crater it cools in place, forming spectacular columnar jointing. Cooling begins at the semicircular base of the crater, and prisms form at right angles to this surface. The convergent rock columns curve as they rise from the bottom of the lava lake, and as a whole they create a graceful sheaf of stone.

Viscous Lavas: Domes and Petaloid Flows

Lavas that erupt at fairly low temperatures, 1,650 degrees Fahrenheit (900 degrees Celsius) or less, are usually very viscous, with a consistency similar to modeling clay or warm asphalt. As a result, they do not flow easily and tend to build up steep-sided,

As lava cools and contracts, it often forms joint-bounded columns, and usually these columns are hexagonal.

fairly symmetrical domes. Large glowing blocks often crack off the summit and roll down the steep sides of these volcanoes. Flows, where present, are very short, up to 1,000 feet (about 300 meters), and have difficulty flowing down the slopes because of the speed at which their flow fronts become chilled and rigid. The pasty lavas that follow are forced to flow to the side of the chilled flow front, which gives the lava a flower-petal pattern when viewed from above. Petaloid flows like this can be found at Peak of Teide on the island of Tenerife in the Canary Islands. These extremely slow flows do not present a danger to people; however, collapses and explosions of viscous domes often result in devastating *nuées ardentes*, French for "glowing avalanches," which can cause destruction even far from a volcano. These dense pyroclastic flows—mixtures of hot gases, ash, and rock—make viscous volcanoes extremely dangerous.

Simple Domes, Complex Domes, and Cryptodomes

Domes of viscous lava may be constructed directly from a fissure in the basement rock. The Puy de Dôme, in the Chaîne des Puys volcanic province in France, grew this way around ten thousand years ago. A mass of viscous lava rose about 1,650 feet (500 meters) above the surrounding plain, collapsing here and there as debris flows. Domes that develop from single eruptions are called *simple domes*. Once the magma ceases to flow into a volcano, the dome stops growing. In some cases the sporadic intrusion of magma may continue over a period of hundreds or thousands of years. Successive lava flows build up gigantic cones with an active dome crowning the summit, giving rise to regular avalanches of blocks down its steep sides. Colima in Mexico and Merapi in Indonesia are examples of large volcanoes that are still growing. Complex domes like these are composed of an interlayering of old domes and their collapse products. Sometimes new domes within an existing volcanic cone do not reach the surface. Instead they stay hidden in a volcano's flanks and are called *cryptodomes*. Cryptodomes can cause a volcano's flanks to inflate, often leading to the volcano's destabilization and collapse.

Growth of domes may be very rapid, as at Mount Pelée on the island of Martinique of the Lesser Antilles, where the mineralogist Alfred Lacroix witnessed a lava needle grow about 750 feet (230 meters) high in a few days before it crumbled catastrophically. For reasons that will be made clear later on, very rapid input of pasty magma into a volcano can lead to devastating explosions, as was the case with the explosion of Mount St. Helens in 1980. After such a powerful eruption, a vast horseshoe-shaped crater is left. If fresh magma feeds the volcano again, it forms new domes that progressively rebuild a new volcanic cone.

Tarumai, Japon

Viscous lavas tend to build up steep-sided, fairly symmetrical domes.

Prismatic Columns in Viscous Lava

Columnar jointing is generally much less spectacular in viscous lavas than in fluid lavas since fluid lavas chill more quickly. The columns that do form from viscous lava are usually broader and more irregular in form; the consistency and quality of the polygonal jointing of the columns varies in inverse proportion to the viscosity of the lava. Columnar jointing in viscous domes fans inward from the outer curved surface of the dome, where the lava started cooling first, as in lava lakes. Examples of this jointing occur at la Roche Sanadoire in the Mont-Dore Massif of central France and at Mont Gerbier de Jonc, the headwaters of the Loire River in France.

VOLCANIC EJECTA

Explosions are spectacular aspects of volcanic activity. They vary from glowing fireworks to threatening plumes of ash that obscure the sun. Eruptions play an important role in the physical makeup of a volcano, but violent eruptions can also result in its partial, or total, destruction. The diverse material volcanoes throw out, up to a great height above a crater, is called *volcanic ejecta*.

Bombs, Lapilli, and Ash

During explosive eruptions, lava fragments of different sizes can become airborne. Larger blobs of lava, either fluid or viscous, are called *volcanic bombs*. Sometimes they are molded during their flight through the atmosphere and fall back to the earth as spindle-shaped fragments called *spindle bombs*. Bombs may also hit the ground and flatten like pancakes; these are called *cowpat bombs*. Viscous lava forms bombs with cracked upper surfaces; they resemble well-baked bread and are called *bread crust bombs*. Smaller fragments, $\frac{5}{64}$ inch to $2\frac{1}{2}$ inches (2 to 64 millimeters) in diameter, are called *lapilli*. These small pieces of lava, or even individual crystals of different minerals, fall like rain on the flanks of a volcanic cone. Ash particles, which are less than $\frac{5}{64}$ inch

(2 millimeters) in diameter, are often dispersed far from a volcanic vent since they are light enough to be carried by the wind.

Inclusions or Xenoliths

Explosive eruptions can also eject fragments of solid rock in variable quantities. These fragments may be extracted from the cone itself (pieces of cooled and solidified lava from a previous eruption), from basement rock (limestone, granite, schist, granulite, etc.) of the earth's crust, or from the mantle more than 25 miles (40 kilometers) below the surface (peridotite, a rock containing a large percentage of the mineral olivine). Kimberlite pipes, volcanoes with magma that originated deep in the earth's mantle, have brought rocks containing diamonds to the surface, which we know form at great depth, up to 250 miles (400 kilometers) below the surface. All these rocks are foreign to the lava actively being erupted from a volcano and are known as *inclusions*, or *xenoliths*.

Pyroclastic Formations

A large proportion of volcanic ejecta falls close to the vent it was ejected from. It forms the pyroclastic (from the Greek *pyro* for "fire" and *klastos* for "broken") deposits that help construct a volcanic cone. Finer-grained ejecta can also accumulate far from the volcano itself. Ejecta is more stratified, or made of easily distinguishable layers, the further it is deposited from a volcano. Close to a vent, larger bombs accumulate and form a poorly sorted and stratified scoria cone, a simple volcano composed of rough, vesicular scoria bombs. Further away from a vent, coherent, well-stratified layers of lapilli and ash accumulate. Bombs and lapilli usually chill and solidify when they come into contact with air, and they are deposited as loose accumulations. However, if they are still incandescent when they fall back down to the ground, the hot fragments can press together, forming welded scoria and tuff deposits. Cones composed of welded scoria and tuff are generally characterized by steep slopes. The finest ash fragments are carried high into the

cauliflower bomb

cowpat bomb

bread crust bomb

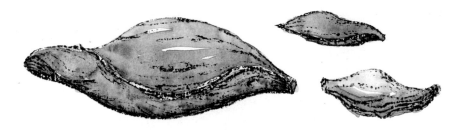

spindle bomb

volcanic bombs

4 inches
(10 cm)

Airborne fragments of lava, either fluid or viscous, can form volcanic bombs.

atmosphere and fall back to the earth far from the volcano, forming ash layers, also called *cinderites*. Cinderites, which are easy to recognize by their mineralogical and chemical features, are frequently interlayered at the bottom of lakes and seas. During the most powerful eruptions, ash can reach altitudes of over 65,000 feet (about 20,000 meters), well into the stratosphere. Ash at this altitude falls back to the earth very slowly over the whole globe.

Dense clouds of coarser blocks—mixed with gas and very hot particles—form at the bottom of explosive ejecta. These clouds travel down the slopes of a volcano at very high speeds, destroying everything in their path. They tend to follow valley features, but frequently they flow over the higher regions that define a valley. Volcanologists recognize different flow types by the abundance of suspended particles. Very dense flows are called *pyroclastic flows*, and less dense flows that are more turbulent are called *surges*. Sometimes these flows create deposits that are welded because they are very hot; other times they blanket slopes with loose deposits.

Ignimbrites

The sudden emptying of a magma chamber containing magma rich in silica and water gives rise to thick, 100- to 130-foot (30- to 40-meter) layers of ignimbrite—the deposits of nuées ardentes—that cover the flanks of a volcano and fill in adjacent valleys. Ignimbrites are poorly sorted deposits with ejecta that range in size. These deposits, which are sometimes pumice rich, can cover an area larger than 10 square miles (about 25 square kilometers). At the time of eruption, layers of ignimbrite close to a vent are often still very hot, and the fragments of bubble-rich volcanic glass that the layers contain may become welded after deposition. A couple of miles (a few kilometers) beyond a vent, the glassy fragments no longer form a coherent welded mass since they cooled rapidly during their journey through the air.

Ignimbrite layers are found around many old volcanoes. They occur around the Mont-Dore Massif in central France, a great mountainous plateau, and in and around Yellowstone National Park. There have been no recent cataclysmic eruptions comparable to those of prehistoric times, which were characterized by the eruption of more than 100 cubic miles (about 400 cubic kilometers) of ignimbrite; however, the eruptions of the Novarupta Volcano in the Katmai area of Alaska in 1912, Mount St. Helens in 1980, and Mount Pinatubo in the Philippines in 1991 did produce sizable ignimbrites.

WHY EXPLOSIVE ERUPTIONS OCCUR

Explosive volcanic eruptions result from a sudden expansion of gas. They occur for two main reasons: magma contains dissolved gas, and rising magma can meet groundwater and cause it to expand in the earth.

Volcanic Gases

Volcanoes send huge amounts of gas into the atmosphere during eruptions, but they also give off gas almost continuously between eruptions. Mount Etna in Sicily emits around 77 million tons (70 million metric tons) of gas per year, which is equal to the mass of lava erupted by the volcano over the same length of time. The figures are slightly different for Merapi in Indonesia, which emits 96 million tons (87 million metric tons) of gas, as well as 220 million tons (200 million metric tons) of rock per year. Worldwide, volcanoes give off around 1.1 billion tons (1 billion metric tons) of gas per year, although this figure is an approximation that varies greatly from year to year.

Volcanic gas is mainly composed of water vapor (80 percent for Mount Etna, nearly 90 percent for Merapi), which forms beautiful white plumes. The remaining gas is carbon dioxide, which is invisible but very toxic when present in large quantities; methane, which is much less dense than air and is quickly carried to high altitudes; sulfur compounds, which smell of rotten eggs; hydrochloric acid and hydrofluoric acid, which burn the eyes and throat; and nitrogen. Gas proportions are significantly different from one volcano to another. The gas emitted from Nyiragongo in the Democratic Republic of the Congo (formerly Zaire) is characterized by a great concentration of carbon dioxide (more than 45 percent), whereas the gas emitted by Kilauea Crater in Hawai'i is especially rich in sulfur dioxide (more than 15 percent).

Other gases occur in tiny quantities, but they can be of interest to geologists. For example, noble gases are very useful, especially argon, which is used to date lavas. The gas of a volcano also contains helium, which is mainly derived from the earth's mantle, and radon, which is continuously produced by the radioactive decay of uranium and thorium.

Volcanic gas also transports a large amount of chemical elements in the form of various salts. Volcanologists have studied the gas output at Mount Etna in detail, and they know that the volcano annually emits 400 tons (about 360 metric tons) of copper, 140 tons (about 130 metric tons) of lead, 30 tons (27 metric tons) of mercury, and 1,540 pounds (about 700 kilograms) of gold into the atmosphere! The gas from Mount Etna is a sizeable atmospheric pollutant, containing five hundred times the level of lead found in the air above central Paris before lead-free fuel was introduced.

Gas Expansion

Deep beneath a volcano, gas is dissolved in the magma rather than forming separate gas bubbles. A good analogy is carbon dioxide dissolved in sparkling mineral water while the bottle is sealed. As soon as someone opens the bottle, the pressure drops suddenly as it equilibrates with surrounding atmospheric pressure. The carbon dioxide that was dissolved in the water is liberated. It forms bubbles that quickly rise toward the surface since the gas is much less dense than water. If the dissolved gas is abundant, a great number of bubbles form and rise, carrying the surrounding liquid with them and causing it to spill out of the bottle. In the same way, when magma rises from deep within the earth to the surface, the pressure decreases markedly. Dissolved gas is liberated and forms bubbles, which grow and multiply in a process known as *vesiculation*. The overall volume of magma and gas increases significantly, often triggering an eruption.

Strombolian Eruptions and Lava Fountains

Volcanoes that emit fluid lavas are characterized by regular explosions at intervals of a few seconds to a few hours. A good example is Stromboli, a volcanic island near Sicily.

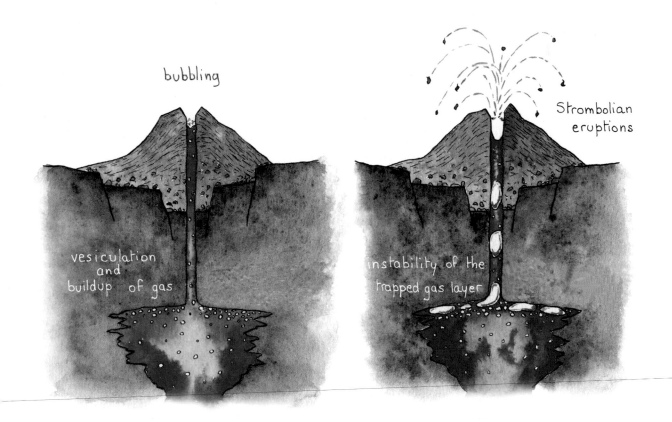

As magma rises toward the surface and pressure drops, its dissolved gas is liberated and forms bubbles, which grow and multiply in a process known as vesiculation.

Sometimes gas and lava are thrown out of a feeder pipe as permanent jets called lava fountains.

When vesiculation takes place in a magma chamber, small bubbles form and rise toward the roof of the chamber, where they remain trapped. At the roof the bubbles combine, forming progressively larger gas bubbles. Once they grow to a certain size, they rush to the bottom of a vent's feeder pipe. These huge bubbles of 50 to 100 cubic feet (several cubic meters) or more rise through the lava of the feeder pipe up to the vent. The difference between the internal pressure of the bubbles and external pressure increases a lot as the gas rises because the external pressure decreases the closer the bubbles get to the earth's surface. As a result, the gas undergoes extreme expansion at the vent, causing the bubbles to explode and throw lava into the air. These Strombolian eruptions are characterized by incandescent lava being thrown up to 650 feet (about 200 meters) above the vent, sometimes faster than the speed of sound. Sometimes the propagation of gas bubbles within a feeder pipe happens almost continuously, and gas and lava are thrown out as permanent jets called *lava fountains*. You can see beautiful and noisy eruptions of this type at Mount Etna in Sicily, at Piton de la Fournaise on Réunion Island off the east coast of Madagascar, and on the island of Hawai'i.

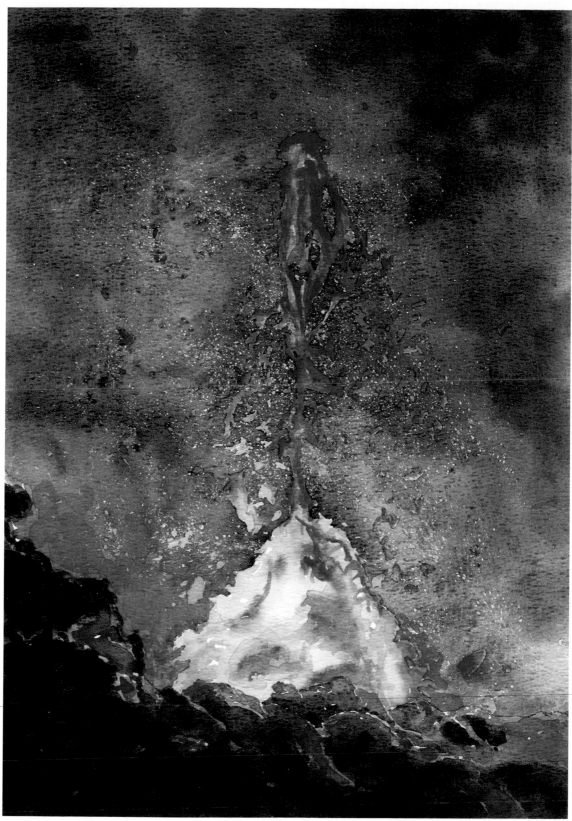

Extreme gas expansion at the vent causes gas bubbles to explode in Strombolian eruptions.

Plinian Eruptions

The sight of viscous and gas-rich magma erupting at the surface is magnificent, but it is safer to watch these explosions from far away since they are often dramatic. It is more difficult for bubbles to form at depth in a magma chamber if the magma has a higher viscosity, so vesiculation cannot take place, or is incomplete, causing the gas to remain dissolved in the ascending magma. Near the surface, gas pressure in the lava is very high, much higher than the external pressure. Sudden, extreme vesiculation transforms the lava into pumice, a highly vesicular rock with such a low density that it often floats on water. The violence of an explosion pulverizes this frothy pumice into small pieces. A turbulent column of gas, carrying ash and pumice fragments in suspension, rises above a volcano throughout an eruption of this type, forming a huge gray cloud, or plume, that resembles a mushroom cloud. This plume, which is characteristic of a Plinian eruption, can rise to an altitude of more than 65,000 feet (about 20,000 meters), where it spreads out laterally in the stratosphere and is distributed by the dominant winds. The particles fall back to the earth over a huge area like rain, creating deposits that are increasingly fine grained away from the crater. An eruption of this type from Mount Vesuvius buried Pompeii in AD 79, suffocating, amongst many others, the Roman scholar Pliny the Elder.

Peléan Eruptions

The rate of dome growth during the eruption of viscous lava determines how efficiently the magma degasses. Where growth is relatively slow, around 100 cubic feet (about 3 cubic meters) per second, the dome regularly collapses in the form of debris avalanches, which are not very dangerous. If, however, the dome is built up fast, more than 350 cubic feet (about 10 cubic meters) per second, the magma does not have enough time to degas; it erupts explosively due to the buildup of pressure,

A turbulent column of gas, carrying ash and pumice fragments in suspension, rises above a volcano, forming a huge gray cloud during a Plinian eruption.

If magma doesn't have enough time to sufficiently degas, a volcano can erupt violently, triggering pyroclastic flows and surges.

triggering pyroclastic flows and surges. These eruptions, termed *Peléan*, occur unpredictably when a dome is fed large amounts of magma.

In 1999 the Soufrière Hills on the island of Montserrat in the Lesser Antilles erupted spectacularly with nuées ardentes that completely destroyed the capital city of Plymouth. A nuée ardente flowing off Mount Pelée laid waste to St. Pierre on nearby Martinique on May 8, 1902, killing twenty-eight thousand people. In 1991 a Peléan eruption at Mount Unzen in Japan killed forty-three people, including three volcanologists—Maurice and Katia Krafft of France and Henry Glicken of the United States.

Surges

The sudden expansion of gas in viscous lavas does not always result in vertical eruptions. Sometimes, depending on the shape and structure of the volcano, the eruption is directed obliquely, or even horizontally, unleashing a powerful blast that destroys everything in its path. One such blast, or surge, laid waste to the slopes and surroundings of Mount St. Helens in 1980, following the collapse of one of the mountain's flanks. Evidence of surges can also be seen on the flanks of numerous volcanoes in the Antilles and in the Pacific Ring of Fire, which is a concentration of volcanoes that roughly circles the Pacific Ocean basin and contains 75 percent of the world's active volcanoes.

When Rising Magma Meets Groundwater

The upper part of the earth's crust is generally saturated with water. This water is mainly rainwater that has percolated down through the soil. It accumulates in the ground, forming reservoirs, and is known as *phreatic water* or, more commonly, *groundwater*. Wells and springs originate from this horizon. Very small pores in the soil and rocks hold the water, and the pores themselves tend to be interconnected by very thin channels. When hot magma rises toward the surface, it often encounters this phreatic water. The water is heated and changes to vapor. Its volume increases a thousandfold, causing the pores holding the water to explode, and the surrounding basement rock breaks apart. Repeated jets of steam, strong enough to carry a significant quantity of rock debris, burst out of the basement rock in a characteristic cypress tree shape. Successive explosions dig deeply into the basement rocks, creating a wide, shallow crater. Circular pyroclastic deposits called *tuff rings* develop around the crater. The deposits are characterized by an abundance of basement rock fragments, as well as a range of fragment sizes that lack significant sorting. A tuff ring generally experiences several stages of building and partial destruction during a single eruption as blast after blast occurs.

The physical results of phreatic eruptions—low-relief, shallow, broad craters surrounded by a ring of debris—are known as *maars*. Craters of this type are found in the Eifel district of Germany, and U.S. examples include the Coliseum maar in the Hopi Buttes volcanic region in northeastern Arizona, and the Ukinrek maars on the Alaska Peninsula. When lava accompanies the jets of water vapor, the eruption is called *phreatomagmatic*. These eruptions are characterized by the formation of cauliflower bombs,

Surtsey, 1963

A phreatic eruption has a characteristic cypress tree shaped plume.

which are blocks of lava that develop an uneven surface as they chill in contact with the water. Maar craters often fill with water over time.

If a large amount of lava continues to be fed to the surface, the phreatic water is exhausted and the jets of water vapor cease. The eruption is then solely magmatic, and the volcanic eruptions are mainly controlled by the expansion of gas bubbles forming in the rising magma, as described for Strombolian eruptions. Strombolian cones—sharp volcanic cones resulting from an accumulation of bombs and lapilli—often develop over maar craters, or even in the center of the maar itself, as in the Maar de Beaunit in the Chaîne des Puys volcanic province in central France.

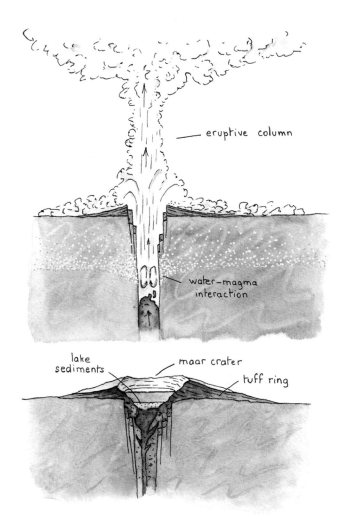

Repeated jets of steam, strong enough to carry a significant quantity of rock debris, burst out of the ground during phreatic eruptions and create a maar.

Phreatic and phreatomagmatic eruptions also occur when lava comes into contact with ice, for example on the summits of the high volcanoes in the Andean Cordillera, or in the glacial regions close to the polar circles, such as in Iceland, Alaska, and Antarctica. They can also occur at shallow depths in the sea—at greater depth the pressure exerted by the water counterbalances the expansion of gas in the magma. The island of Surtsey, off Iceland's south coast, grew from an underwater volcano starting in 1963.

CARBONIC ERUPTIONS

Three fairly recent catastrophes have shown that some volcanic systems, such as fissure zones and crater lakes, give off large amounts of carbon dioxide. Since carbon dioxide is denser than air, gravity pulls it down valleys before winds disperse the gas in the atmosphere. Above a certain concentration in the air (10 to 20 percent), carbon dioxide is lethal, and these emissions have caused a great number of deaths: 149 at Dieng Volcano in Java, Indonesia, in 1979; 37 at Lake Monoun in Cameroon in 1984; and 1,750 around Lake Nyos in Cameroon in 1986.

Percolation of Carbon Dioxide through Earth's Crust

In some regions around the world, carbon dioxide diffuses from deep in the earth to the surface. In the Auvergne region of France, for instance, on rainy days you can see bubbles of carbon dioxide rising from puddles in the streets of the town of St. Nectaire. Carbon dioxide is very soluble in water, increasingly so under high pressure and at low temperatures. When a flux of carbon dioxide rises into deep water reservoirs or aquifers, sizeable quantities of the gas can be dissolved in the water, and as the gas-rich water approaches the reduced pressure of the surface, the gas expands substantially. If these gas-rich waters rise gradually to the surface, they can feed springs of sparkling carbonic water. The near-surface release of carbon dioxide in calcium-rich waters leads to the precipitation of limestone around a vent; these formations are called *petrifying springs*, of which Mammoth Hot Springs in Yellowstone National Park is a famous example.

Disruption of Deep Aquifer Layers

Two variables can disrupt carbon dioxide–rich aquifers and lead to the release of carbon dioxide at the surface: a lowering of pressure or a rise in temperature. In both cases the solubility of carbon dioxide decreases and a portion of it that was previously in solution is freed. If access is available, the carbon dioxide rushes to the surface. Volcanologists believe that a minor volcanic eruption at Dieng Volcano heated a carbon dioxide–rich aquifer, which was suddenly decompressed when an earthquake-related fissure opened.

Overturn of Water in Crater Lakes

Some lakes are fed by carbon dioxide–rich springs, or they dissolve carbon dioxide that percolates up from below the lake bottom. The comparatively denser, carbon dioxide–rich water naturally stagnates in the bottom of the lake. Lakes, however, are frequently vigorously stirred by rainfall and wind, and carbon dioxide is released close to the surface and is ultimately mixed with air in the atmosphere.

Crater lakes, though, are an exception due to their physical form: they are very deep for their surface area and tend to have steep sides. They often retain a layer of water at depth that is not mixed with the other water, and in which high levels of methane and carbon dioxide tend to concentrate. Sometimes these lakes release carbon dioxide sud-

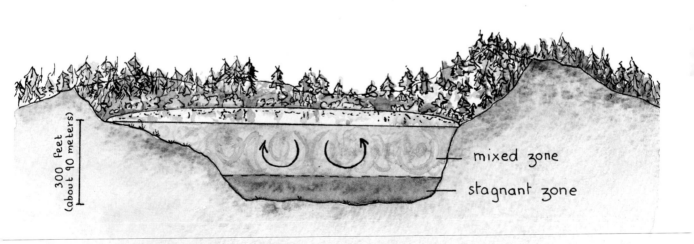

Crater lakes often retain a layer of water at depth where methane and carbon dioxide can become concentrated because the layer is not mixed with the water above.

denly without any volcanic event. For example, a disturbance of a lake, such as the collapse of a cliff on its bank, may stir its deep water and cause it to rapidly rise to the surface. Such "overturning" of a lake has been suggested for the gaseous eruptions of Lakes Monoun and Nyos in Cameroon, although some volcanologists deduce that the gas was released because of a volcanic event. During the 1986 disaster at Lake Nyos, close to 3.5 billion cubic feet (100 million cubic meters) of gas was suddenly liberated.

The Auvergne region of France is home to a crater lake deep enough to have established an isolated layer of water at depth: Lac Pavin has an inert layer between the depth of 200 feet (about 60 meters) and the bottom at 300 feet (about 90 meters). In this volume of water, there could be up to 2.5 billion cubic feet (about 70 million cubic meters) of carbon dioxide threatening the nearby town of Besse en Chandesse. However, recent analyses show that the actual quantity of carbon dioxide in this deep layer is very low.

THE EFFECTS OF VOLCANIC ERUPTIONS ON CLIMATE

Large Plinian or Peléan volcanic eruptions can obscure the sunlight for some time, resulting in a measurable decrease in average temperature at the earth's surface. The climatic effects of the 1980 eruption of Mount St. Helens continued for a year, with an average decrease in temperature of 1.8 degrees Fahrenheit (1 degree Celsius). The catastrophic eruption of Krakatoa in the Indian Ocean in 1883 presumably had similar effects. The huge eruption of Santorini—a volcanic island in the Aegean Sea—around 1500 BC, which destroyed the Minoan civilization, probably had a disastrous climatic effect on agriculture as far away as the Nile Valley; perhaps the Old Testament story of the seven thin cows (corresponding to seven successive years of poor harvests and famine) refers to this event.

Geologists have proposed that intense, continuous volcanism (over several hundred thousand years) may have caused extinction events in the past. If true, the dinosaurs had two excellent reasons to disappear from the earth's surface 65 million years ago: they experienced both the huge impact of the Chicxulub meteorite, which fell in the present-day Gulf of Mexico and sent a great deal of dust into the atmosphere, and the effect of a million years of very strong volcanic activity in northwest India, which created the widespread, flat-lying volcanic terrain called the Deccan Traps and also pumped enormous amounts of gas and dust into the atmosphere.

REPOSE PERIOD OF A VOLCANO AND FUMAROLIC ACTIVITY

Once magma has lost part of its gas through vesiculation, further degassing proceeds more calmly, without major explosions or eruptions. Fumarolic activity, where trails of vapor escape either from a crater itself or from fissures around a volcanic cone, characterizes this state of repose. The vapors contain dissolved salts that are deposited along fissures, notably in the form of yellow sulfur and white sulfates. The vapor released by fumaroles is only partly related to magma degassing; fumaroles are predominantly fed by rainwater, which percolates down through the permeable volcanic deposits and vaporizes at depth because of continuing high temperatures. Bubbling mud and geysers, collectively known as *solfataras*, also characterize the typical dormant volcanic landscape.

SUBMARINE VOLCANOES: ERUPTIONS BENEATH THE SEA

The seafloor is composed almost entirely of a thick basalt layer. Submarine volcanic eruptions account for almost two-thirds of the lavas found on the earth. No one has ever seen a deep-sea eruption or witnessed its effects at the ocean's surface because there are no visible signs of these eruptions—gas is not released at great depth. Nevertheless, over the last thirty years volcanologists have studied the products of these deep-sea eruptions using specially adapted submarines, such as the American submersible *Alvin* and the French submersibles *Cyana* and *Nautile*. Numerous rock-collecting expeditions using dredging and core drilling techniques, as well as the submersibles, have supplied volcanologists with a variety of deep-sea rocks to analyze.

Hyaloclastites

At shallow depths, up to 2,000 to 2,300 feet (about 600 to 700 meters), water pressure is low enough that vesiculation occurs in underwater lava and seawater vaporizes when it comes into contact with magma. This results in very violent phreatomagmatic eruptions in which the magma is broken up into fragments, typically thin needles several millimeters in length. These fragments vitrify (convert into glass) immediately upon contact with the cold seawater. The distinctive deposit of loose fragments that is the result of such eruptions is called a *hyaloclastite*, from the Greek *hyalinos* for "glass" and *klastos* for "broken."

Pillow Lavas and Lava Ponds

At greater depths, particularly along mid-ocean ridges at depths of around 8,200 feet (2,500 meters), the pressure of the seawater prevents the expansion of gas and its accompanying explosive eruptions. Instead, the lavas are extruded gently and fall into two main morphological types: pillow lavas and lava ponds.

Pillow lavas are extruded from fissures that parallel mid-ocean ridges. They are rounded or ovoid lava formations up to 10 feet (3 meters) across. Small volcanoes constructed of pillows and associated elongated tubes piled on top of each other can have very steep sides (up to 60 degrees!). Pillows and tubes develop polygonal columnar joints, as found in eruptions on dry land, due to contraction along the magma's cooling surfaces. Because the surfaces of these formations are very curved, the polygonal columns form a radial or fanlike pattern instead of straight columns. These pillow and tube formations can extend up to 2 miles (about 3 kilometers).

The formation of pillow lavas has been filmed on the island of Hawai'i, at the point where flows that originated on dry land reach the sea. The lava, at about 2,200 degrees Fahrenheit (1,200 degrees Celsius), is immediately quenched upon contact with the rather cool seawater, about 40 degrees Fahrenheit (4 degrees Celsius) at a depth of 8,200 feet (2,500 meters); a thin glassy crust, about ⅜ to ¾ inch (1 to 2 centimeters) thick, forms at the end of the lava tubes and pillows, effectively plugging them. Pressure exerted by the magma trapped in the tube or pillow causes the glass crust to break, and a new tube or pillow emerges and chills. The length of a pillow or tube depends on the angle of the slope onto which the lava is extruded. The cycle continues, with the pillows and tubes piling on top of each other and the gaps filled by glassy debris. In addition to marine environments, pillows and tubes can also form in lakes located in volcanically active areas.

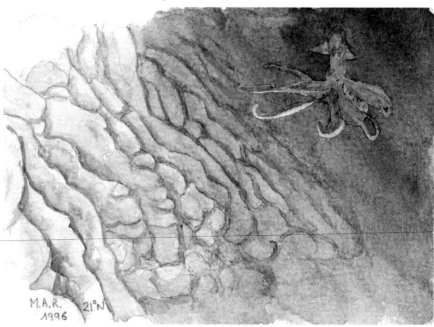

Pillow lavas are rounded or ovoid formations.

Pillars of solidified basalt develop around jets of superheated seawater that rise through underwater lava ponds.

Large volumes of basalt can build up in depressions in the submarine topography, forming lava ponds. Their surface is smooth or sometimes draped and can cover an area of ¾ square mile or more (2 or more square kilometers). Beneath the thin, glassy crust the lava cools slowly and remains liquid for a long time. Pillars of solidified basalt develop around jets of superheated seawater. Initially, seawater is trapped beneath a lava pond, but it moves up through the pond as geysers. The molten lava close to the geysers chills and hardens. When lava ponds occur adjacent to mid-ocean ridges, the lava is often pulled laterally due to tectonic activity, escaping the lava pond as fluid lava flows. The surface of these flows may be ropy or draped, and they may develop impressive columnar jointing like lava flows on dry land. Once the glassy crust collapses above these emptied lava ponds, they are reduced to a field of crumbling pillars, which radiate a strange, otherworldly beauty.

Black Smokers

Deep-sea hydrothermal vents known as *black smokers* are another consequence of submarine volcanism. Basalt lavas on the seafloor contract and crack while chilling and are also fractured by faults that are caused by tectonic movement along mid-ocean ridges. These fractures provide easy access for seawater to penetrate down into a lava pile—to depths of 2 miles (about 3 kilometers) or so. At this depth the water is near the roof of the shallow magma chamber that supplies the seafloor with its basaltic lavas, and it becomes heated to temperatures between 660 and 750 degrees Fahrenheit (about 350 and 400 degrees Celsius). As the heated water moves back up through the lava pile, it alters the rocks and becomes enriched in metallic elements such as iron, copper, zinc, and manganese, as well as sulfur. Some of this enriched fluid remains trapped as brines within the permeable lava pile, but the less dense portion rises toward the seafloor to feed hydrothermal springs at a temperature of about 660 degrees Fahrenheit (350 degrees Celsius). These black smokers construct chimneys of plain sulfide minerals such as pyrite, chalcopyrite, and sphalerite. The name *black smoker* is a reference to the fine particulates of black sulfide minerals that form in the hot water; the formation looks like a smokestack spewing black smoke.

The area surrounding these chimneys are deep-sea oases of life where very unusual organisms flourish, such as 10-foot-long (3-meter-long) giant worms and highly populous clam colonies. At the lower end

When the glassy crust of an emptied lava pond collapses, it leaves a field of crumbling pillars.

Hydrothermal springs jet from lava piles and construct chimneys of sulfide minerals, so-called black smokers.

of the food chain there are unusual heat-loving bacteria that thrive because of the high temperatures. Black smokers, and their surrounding fauna, are very important scientifically and philosophically. Many scientists deduce that they replicate the conditions under which life first developed on Earth over 3 billion years ago.

VOLCANIC COLLAPSE

The shape of volcanoes and the relief of volcanic landscapes are not simply due to volcanic eruptions and their products (lava and pyroclastic deposits). Gravity also plays a major role in reshaping volcanic contours, not only during eruptions, but also in periods of dormancy and even after volcanic activity has ceased entirely.

Lahars

The destabilization of a volcano's flanks may be triggered by eruptions: for example, devastating nuées ardentes are the result of the collapse of hot, glowing domes that have not fully degassed. However, other factors can cause flanks to destabilize. Pyroclastic debris on a volcano's flanks, when it is unwelded, is usually fairly unstable. Slides of pyroclastic debris are often as catastrophic for the environment, and for humans, as eruptions themselves. Mudflows, or *lahars* (the Indonesian word for "mudflow"), generally occur where layers of volcanic ash were deposited on a volcano's flanks during its initial phase of explosive activity. Saturated by heavy tropical rainfall or by glacial meltwaters from the summit of the volcano, the ash is transformed into a thick mud. This mud reaches flow speeds of up to 90 miles per hour (145 kilometers per hour) down a volcano's flanks, fills valleys, and even climbs up hillsides in some cases. The density and momentum of lahars allows them to pick up very large blocks of rock that they encounter, and to tear down everything in their way, including vegetation and buildings.

A lahar that occurred in Colombia in 1985 exemplifies the utter devastation one can wreak. This lahar originated at the volcano Nevado del Ruiz and completely destroyed portions of the town of Armero 47 miles (75 kilometers) away. In total, twenty-three thousand people died. Lahars also swept down Mount St. Helens following the 1980 eruption.

Flank Slides

Volcano instability is not restricted to a thin layer of superficial pyroclastic deposits; whole sections of a volcanic cone can collapse due to gravity. Old slides involving a very large mass of rock, on the order of 1 cubic mile (4 cubic kilometers), are clearly traceable on many volcanoes: the Valle del Bove on Mount Etna in Sicily, Grand Brulé on Piton de la Fournaise on Réunion Island, and on Peak of Teide on the island of Tenerife in the Canary Islands. Such large-scale slips are facilitated by, or even triggered by, magmatic activity. The intrusion of a large volume of magma into a volcanic cone can critically destabilize its structure. This was the case at Mount St. Helens, where a cryptodome of viscous lava developed within the volcano, causing the northern flank to bulge and become unstable. This brought about the sudden collapse of the cone, producing a horseshoe-shaped depression, and the instantaneous drop in pressure caused the magma to explode violently in a lateral blast. The ensuing nuée ardente reached speeds of almost 680 miles per hour (about 1,100 kilometers per hour), and since it was also very hot, around 570 degrees Fahrenheit (300 degrees Celsius), it left a trail

0.6 mile
(1 km)

The intrusion of magma can destabilize a volcano's cone and cause it to collapse, which leads to an instantaneous drop in pressure and a violent lateral eruption.

of destruction over 18 miles (about 30 kilometers) long and killed fifty-seven people. Even today one can still see the trees that were knocked down in alignment with the direction of the blast, bearing witness to the power of the explosion. Together with lahars, which followed the dramatic explosion, the blast transformed the picturesque volcanic landscape into a desolate place.

Calderas

Huge cataclysmic eruptions can almost completely empty a magma chamber, leaving the roof of the chamber unsupported. This causes the roof to collapse up to a depth of 1 mile (1.6 kilometers) or so, depending on the size of the chamber. In some cases, an entire volcano may be swallowed up by a collapse, leaving a circular or elliptical depression called a *caldera*.

On our planet, one of the biggest calderas—18 miles (about 30 kilometers) long, 9 miles (15 kilometers) wide, and up to 2 miles (about 3 kilometers) deep—that geologists know of is at Long Valley, California. Its huge proportions developed after an eruption, 760,000 years ago, of more than 140 cubic miles (about 600 cubic kilometers) of ignimbrite. The Yellowstone caldera, at 47 miles (75 kilometers) long and 28 miles (45 kilometers) wide, which erupted about 240 cubic miles (about 1,000 cubic kilometers) of ignimbrite 600,000 years ago, is even larger.

The largest caldera in the solar system, though, is the one atop Olympus Mons on Mars. All large calderas on our planet are ancient volcanic structures. The calderas that formed more recently are smaller in size. For example, the caldera of Santorini Island in the Aegean Sea, which formed 3,600 years ago, is 6 miles (10 kilometers) long and 980 feet (about 300 meters) deep; it erupted about 10 cubic miles (40 cubic kilometers) of ignimbrite. Following the 1883 eruption of Krakatoa, a caldera measuring 2½ by 1¼ miles (4 by 2 kilometers) formed. Even more recently, the 1991 eruption of Mount Pinatubo in the Philippines resulted in a caldera that is 2 to 2½ miles (about 3 to 4 kilometers) in diameter.

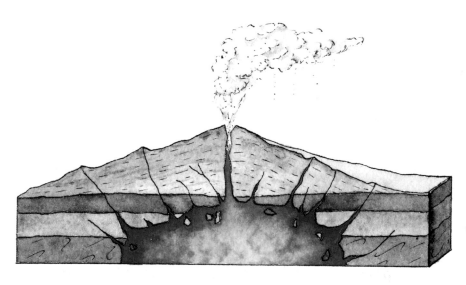

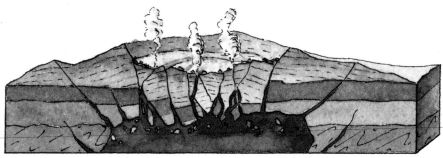

After a cataclysmic eruption the roof of a magma chamber can collapse because it is no longer supported, forming a depression called a caldera.

WHERE MAGMA ORIGINATES

Many people mistakenly believe that the earth is composed of a solid crust, on which we live, resting on a molten mass of rock that makes up the earth's interior. In this scenario, volcanic eruptions would be the result of molten rock escaping the interior and reaching the surface through holes in the crust. This point of view is completely inaccurate and does not reflect the knowledge of the earth's interior that science has collected over the last two centuries. Most of our knowledge of the earth's interior has come from the study of seismic waves that propagate through the earth after earthquakes.

THE EARTH'S CONCENTRIC STRUCTURE

Solid rocks do, in fact, make up the outer layers of the earth, from the surface down to a depth of about 1,796 miles (2,890 kilometers). The outermost skin, called the *crust*, is composed of granite under the continents and basalt under the oceans; it ranges between 3 and 25 miles (5 and 40 kilometers) thick. Beneath this crust lies the *mantle*, a huge mass (80 percent of the earth's volume) of dense rocks, such as peridotite and its high-pressure equivalent deeper in the mantle.

A transition occurs at a depth of 1,796 miles (2,890 kilometers), beyond which certain seismic waves (S waves; also called *shear waves*) cannot propagate. This is the boundary between solid rock and the 1,404-mile-thick (2,260-kilometer-thick) molten layer known as the *outer core*. This molten material is very dense, more than 620 pounds per cubic foot (10 metric tons per cubic meter). It is a metallic alloy composed predominantly of iron with a small amount of nickel. The center of the earth, called the *inner core*, is a solid mass with a radius of 758 miles (1,220 kilometers). It has the same metallic composition as the outer core because it is a crystallized version of the outer core. Geologists deduce that the composition of the earth's core is very similar to the composition of iron meteorites—fragments of ancient small planets—that occasionally crash into the earth.

Corresponding to the concentric structure of the earth, temperature increases from about 32 degrees Fahrenheit (0 degree Celsius) at the surface to approximately 7,200 degrees Fahrenheit (about 4,000 degrees Celsius) at the boundary between the outer core and mantle, which is the temperature of the molten iron-nickel alloy at the pressure of the outer core. Experimental and theoretical studies have shown that the base of the earth's mantle is no hotter than 5,400 degrees Fahrenheit (about 3,000 degrees Celsius), so the boundary between the mantle and the outer core is marked by a sharp increase in temperature of around 1,800 degrees Fahrenheit (about 1,000 degrees Celsius). This temperature increase must occur over a short distance. Pressure also increases with depth since it correlates with the mass of overlying rocks. This very high pressure is what keeps the mantle as solid rock at such high temperatures.

There is a paradox with what is molten rock within the earth and what appears as molten rock at the surface: the only liquid layer in the earth, the outer core, has a metallic composition totally different from the lavas that erupt at the surface. Lavas are composed of silicates or, more rarely, carbonates. The density of the outer core liquid is so great that it would be impossible for it to ever reach the surface. So where

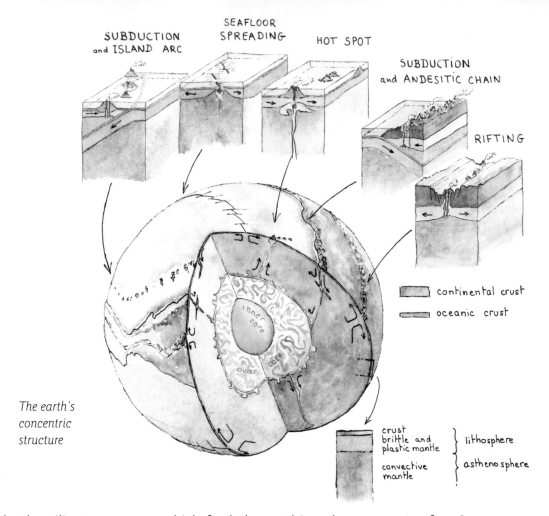

SUBDUCTION and ISLAND ARC

SEAFLOOR SPREADING

HOT SPOT

SUBDUCTION and ANDESITIC CHAIN

RIFTING

The earth's concentric structure

inner core

outer core

continental crust

oceanic crust

crust

brittle and plastic mantle

convective mantle

lithosphere

asthenosphere

do the silicate magmas, which feed the earth's volcanoes, come from? The answer to this question lies in the localized partial melting of the solid mantle layer and the earth's crust.

PARTIAL MELTING OF ROCKS

A solid rock is made up of assemblages of different minerals. Each mineral type is characterized by a very regular arrangement of atoms, which in turn determines the crystal forms (shapes) that individual mineral specimens exemplify. Strictly speaking, minerals are composed of ions rather than atoms. Ions are electrically charged atoms, which have either a positive or negative charge. Ions of different elements have distinct dimensions, and their ionic radii measure just a few angstroms (ten angstroms is one millionth of a millimeter!). Within each crystal the ions are arranged into very compact and regular geometric structures that are electrostatically equilibrated. These crystal structures, as well as the proportions of individual minerals within a rock, are not random; they correspond to the most efficient way, in the context of energy saving, to store the different ions in a rock at a given temperature and pressure. If these conditions change, then the ions rearrange themselves, so that while the chemical composition in a rock remains constant, its constituent minerals may change. Under some physical conditions—for example, if the temperature rises or the pressure lowers—it becomes too costly in terms of energy for the ions to remain in a crystalline structure. The result is that the crystal structure, or the pattern in which the ions are held together, is destroyed and replaced by randomly organized ion groups. In other words, the rock begins to melt.

Of course, a material as complex as a rock does not instantaneously pass from the solid state to the liquid state. There are intermediate states, or degrees of partial melting, in which certain elements (notably those that have the largest ionic radii or form relatively large ionic complexes) are the least stable in a crystalline form. These elements are somewhat incompatible with the solid state under conditions of partial melting, and they are known as *incompatible elements* or *magmaphiles*, since they prefer the liquid, or magmatic, state. These elements leave their crystal structures to form a partial melt, which then coexists with solid crystals made up of those ions that prefer to remain in a crystal lattice. These ions, called *compatible elements*, are generally small in size.

Partial melts do not have the same chemical composition as the initial rock since the melt is relatively enriched in incompatible elements and depleted in compatible elements. Experimental research shows that partial melts extracted from mantle peridotites have the composition of basalt, which is the rock that dominates the oceanic crust, while melts extracted from the continental crust, which is much richer in silica, have the composition of granite or rhyolite.

Migration of a Melt

In small quantities, a partial melt remains trapped in small pores between the crystals of solid rock. If the rate of partial melting increases enough, then the pores enlarge and become interlinked via thin films of magma around individual crystals. At this stage the rock becomes permeable and the melt can flow and migrate away from its site of origin. Since the melt is less dense than the surrounding rock, it rises toward the surface. On reaching an impermeable layer, where partial melting has not taken place or has occurred to a smaller degree, the melt gathers in pockets, which exert pressure on the solid rock above. When enough pressure builds up, hydraulic fracturing of the rock takes place and the melt escapes through newly opened fissures.

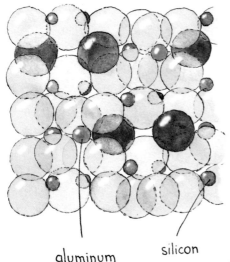

aluminum   silicon

sodium   oxygen

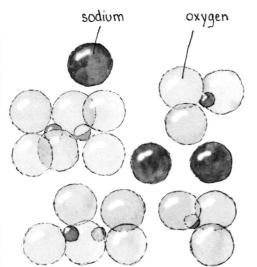

Under certain physical conditions, the crystalline structure of a mineral is destroyed.

Formation of Magma Chambers

Sometimes the difference in the density of solid rock and melt is great enough to propel the melt all the way to the earth's surface, where it erupts as lava. In general, however, hydraulic fracturing is slowed by various rock discontinuities—horizontal changes in rock type or structure. These discontinuities create mechanical boundaries, for example, the boundary between the mantle and the crust. Melt pools at these discontinuities, forming magma reservoirs, or chambers. Once enough magma is injected into a chamber, the rock above is put under enough pressure to cause hydraulic fracturing. The melt can once again proceed upward, ultimately erupting at the surface.

Near the surface of the earth's crust, in what is called the *brittle zone*, magma is frequently channeled along faults. Sometimes it accumulates in these fractures or along rock discontinuities. Several magma chambers can be stacked more or less vertically between the zone of melt production and the surface.

THE CONDITIONS OF PARTIAL MELTING

Like all solids, above a certain temperature rocks will undergo melting, either partial or complete. However, the melting point of a rock is not a fixed temperature; it rises as pressure increases. As a result, the melting point for rocks deeper in the earth is higher. The melting point of a rock is always lowered when extra substances, including fluids such as water or carbon dioxide,

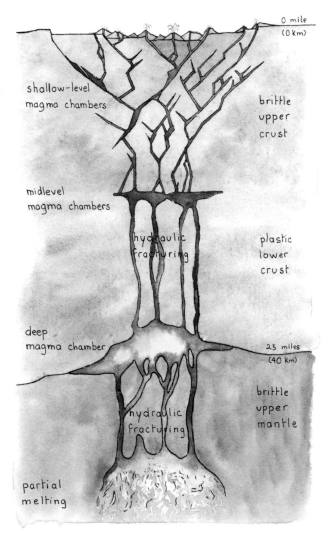

Magma's hydraulic fracturing of rock can be slowed down by various discontinuities— horizontal changes in rock type or structure.

are added to the solid rock. Metallurgists take advantage of this fact by adding flux minerals, such as fluorite and cryolite, to metal alloys in order to lower their melting points. These three factors—relatively high temperature, relatively low pressure, and the fluxing action of water and carbon dioxide—are the reasons why the rocks of the crust and mantle, which seismic waves demonstrate to be generally solid, can undergo partial melting.

MANTLE CONVECTION AND PLATE TECTONICS

Each of the three factors that lead to partial melting are caused by the cooling of the earth, which is an ongoing process that involves convection in the mantle.

The earth's mantle is situated between the very hot core at 7,200 degrees Fahrenheit (about 4,000 degrees Celsius) and the colder layer of rocks at the earth's surface, at about 32 degrees Fahrenheit (0 degree Celsius). Heat is transferred in the mantle, from the core to close to the surface, by the slow, steady convective rise of hot mantle rock. This is the same phenomenon that heats a pot of water on a stove. Initially, the water is heated at the base of the pot, and this warm water expands, consequently decreasing its density. The warmed water then rises, and the overlying cooler water sinks because of gravity. Once the warm water reaches the surface, it cools in contact with the air and becomes denser relative to the underlying warmer water, causing it to sink back to the bottom of the pot again. Convection currents are established in this way, taking the form of fairly regular cells that continue to mix the water until the boiling point is reached.

As rock in the earth's mantle is heated at depth, particularly rock adjacent to the hot outer core, its density is lowered. This causes the rock to slowly rise, up to 1 foot (30 centimeters) or so a year, toward the surface. Near the surface the rock is cooled to such a degree that it loses its plasticity and its density increases again, causing it to sink under the force of gravity.

3/8 to 4 inches (1 to 10 cm) per second

subduction   seafloor spreading

4 inches (10 cm) per year

400 miles (650 km)

Like water in a pot, rocks are heated at depth and rise, while cooler rocks near the surface sink back to depth, creating a convective circulation cell.

Improbable as it may seem to have solid rock flowing up and down in the mantle, research into the physical properties of mantle rocks, such as viscosity and thermal conductivity, confirms that this process is indeed a reality.

Seafloor Spreading

Rocks forming the earth's continents and rocks underlying the earth's ocean basins are called *continental crust* and *oceanic crust*, respectively. The continental and oceanic crust form a coating, or "skin," on top of the earth's mantle. The outermost portion of the mantle together with the overlying crust forms an outer shell that is relatively cold and, consequently, rather rigid. The shell is called the *lithosphere* (rock sphere). The thickness of the lithosphere varies between 50 and 75 miles (80 and 120 kilometers). It is generally much thicker where it includes a continent. The lithosphere sits on the highly plastic and convective part of the mantle called the *asthenosphere* (weak sphere), and the lithosphere is broken up into fragments called *plates*. Over the earth as a whole there are about twelve major lithospheric plates that move laterally, "floating" on the asthenosphere. The study of their movement is called *plate tectonics*. The majority of the earth's seismic and volcanic activity is focused along the boundaries of these plates.

Mantle convection manifests at the earth's surface as the lateral motion of lithospheric plates. For example, North America and Europe, each situated on a separate plate, have been moving apart for more than 120 million years at a rate of up to 2 inches (about 5 centimeters) per year. These plates, like numerous others, are separating because of rising convection currents in the hot, plastic mantle. As the mantle rocks rise, they spread out near the surface beneath the Atlantic Ocean and move laterally away from each other on either side of a submarine mountain belt. This mid-ocean ridge, like other similar ridges, is characterized by strong volcanic activity. It is also characterized by shallow seismic

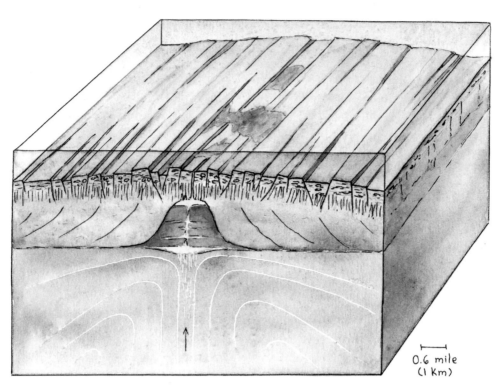

Lithospheric plates at the earth's surface are separating because of rising convection currents in the hot, plastic mantle.

0.6 mile
(1 km)

activity in which the focus of each earthquake is less than 6 miles (10 kilometers) deep. This divergent, lateral movement of oceanic crust is called *seafloor spreading.*

Close to the earth's surface the rising mantle cools below 2,200 degrees Fahrenheit (1,200 degrees Celsius), and it progressively loses its plasticity. As it becomes more rigid, deformation occurs by fracturing, giving rise to seismic activity. The rigid lithospheric plates thicken away from a mid-ocean ridge due to a lateral decrease in temperature away from the convective upwelling. At a distance of 125 miles (200 kilometers) or more from a mid-ocean ridge, a lithospheric plate is around 60 miles (100 kilometers) thick. The upper layer of these plates is composed of oceanic crust—the basaltic magmas that crystallize in or are erupted as lava at mid-ocean ridges.

Subduction

Some parts of the earth's surface, for example, around the edge of the Pacific Ocean, are characterized by deep ocean trenches and seismic activity with earthquake foci as deep as 400 miles (650 kilometers). Arcs of volcanoes are arrayed parallel to each deep ocean trench. Volcanic activity in these volcanic arcs is very intense, as exemplified by the Pacific Ring of Fire, which roughly circles the Pacific Ocean basin and includes the impressive volcanoes of the Andean Cordillera, the Cascades of the Pacific Northwest, and the Aleutian Islands. Deep ocean trenches, and their associated volcanic activity, form when a cold and dense oceanic lithospheric plate slips beneath a more buoyant lithospheric plate (often a plate that includes continental crust) into the hotter, more plastic asthenosphere. This process is known as *subduction*. Subduction zones are located where the cooling lithospheric plates are thick and dense enough to sink back toward the lower mantle, therefore maintaining the convection cell motion.

Detailed research into the propagation of seismic waves through the entire mantle (lithosphere and asthenosphere) reveals that slabs of cooler rock (through which waves propagate relatively quickly) can be detected sloping down into the warmer mantle (through which the waves pass more slowly). These cooler slabs can be found 300 to 400 miles (about 500 to 650 kilometers) deep in the mantle, and occasionally all the way down to the base of the mantle at its boundary with the outer core. The rising and falling arms of convection cells within the mantle correspond, respectively, to mid-ocean ridges and subduction zones. These zones are major sites of mantle partial melting.

MANTLE UPWELLING: PARTIAL MELTING DUE TO REDUCED PRESSURE

In general, rocks—especially mantle peridotites—are poor conductors of heat. Because of this, rocks maintain their heat for a long time, even when

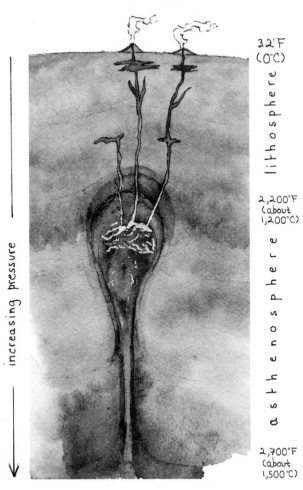

increasing pressure

32°F
(0°C)

lithosphere

2,200°F
(about
1,200°C)

asthenosphere

2,700°F
(about
1,500°C)

Because rocks generally are poor conductors of heat, mantle rocks maintain very high temperatures as they rise to the surface by convection.

introduced into a cooler environment. So even as mantle rocks rise to the surface by convection, they maintain very high temperatures. At the same time, the pressure progressively decreases, and at shallow enough depths partial melting can occur as a result of this decompression.

Formation of the Oceanic Crust

The production of magma through decompressional melting of the mantle fuels the volcanic activity at mid-ocean ridges. The rising convection currents not only push oceanic plates apart, but they also cause the partial melting of peridotites beginning at depths of 25 to 30 miles (40 to 50 kilometers). Huge volumes of magma are produced, up to 20 percent of the mass of the original mantle. The magma collects in small chambers beneath mid-ocean ridges. Magma can crystallize in the chambers, forming a coarse-grained rock called *gabbro*, which has the same chemical composition as basalt. From time to time, a portion of the magma rises to the ocean floor through vertical dikes and is extruded as lava flows or pillow lavas, or it can fill topographic lows with lava ponds. When this magma from the mantle is extruded onto the ocean floor, it forms basalt. It is the layered combination of the gabbros, vertical dikes, and basaltic lava flows that make up the oceanic crust, which is continuously produced at mid-ocean ridges.

The thickness of the crust at mid-ocean ridges reflects the amount of magma formed at depth in the mantle and varies according to the rate of seafloor spreading. A rapid rate of spreading, such as the 3- to 4-inch (8- to 10-centimeter) spread per year that occurs along the East Pacific Rise, which separates the Pacific Plate from those along its eastern edge, corresponds to a rapid ascent of mantle material. This rapid ascent causes high rates of partial melting and the formation of a relatively thick oceanic crust—4 to about 4½ miles (about 6 to 7 kilometers). Where spreading is slower, such as the ⅜- to ¾-inch (1- to 2-centimeter) spread that occurs along the Mid-Atlantic Ridge, the mantle material rises less rapidly; consequently, the rate of partial melting is lower, creating a thinner, often discontinuous crust, about ⅝ to 1¼ miles (1 to 2 kilometers) thick.

Hot Spot Volcanism

Rising convection currents sometimes originate at very great depths, down to the core-mantle boundary. The temperature at these depths can be very high, up to 5,400 degrees Fahrenheit (about 3,000 degrees Celsius), and in spite of the very high pressures, it is likely that this extremely hot mantle is partially molten. With a relatively low viscosity, this hot material rises through the mantle in the form of long plumes. Its voyage to the earth's surface can take millions to tens of millions of years. At a depth of 60 to 90 miles (100 to 150 kilometers), the decompression of such hot material leads to extensive partial melting and the production of magma in the head of the plume (up to 30 percent of its volume). This magma erupts at the surface over a relatively short time period (usually less than 1 million years) and over a relatively limited area geographically. The thick piles of lava are called *flood basalts* and include those in Siberia (250 million years old) and in Ethiopia (30 million years old). One of the largest flood basalt provinces is the Columbia River Plateau in Oregon and Washington; its eruptions began about 17.5 million years ago.

There are no active flood basalts forming at the moment, but there are many hot spots at the earth's surface. After the paroxysmal volcanism related to the partial melting of the plume head ends, the plume tail continues to rise for tens of millions of years, undergoing decompression and partial melting to a lesser degree and feeding volcanoes. Volcanism linked to hot spots is distinctive in that the plume originating deep in the mantle remains stationary while the overlying lithospheric plate continues to move. So volcanoes resulting from hot spot activity trace a line across a lithospheric plate. The line traces a path that is the reverse of the plate movement on the earth's surface. Such volcanism is known as *intraplate volcanism* because it does not occur along plate boundaries like the volcanic activity that occurs along mid-ocean ridges.

A hot spot beneath Réunion Island in the Indian Ocean feeds the active volcanoes of Piton des Neiges and Piton de la Fournaise. Before these volcanoes formed, this same hot spot created the Mauritius Islands 7 to 1 million years ago; the Mascarenes Ridge,

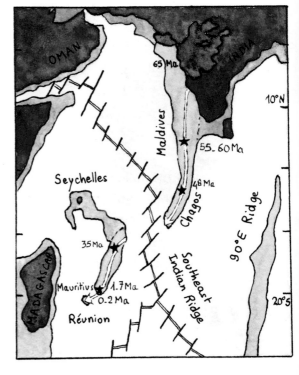

There is a hot spot situated beneath Réunion Island in the Indian Ocean feeding the active volcanoes of Piton de la Fournaise and Piton des Neiges.

a submerged volcanic ridge, 35 million years ago; the Chagos Ridge, another almost completely submerged volcanic ridge, 48 million years ago; and the Maldive Islands 60 million years ago. About 65 million years ago partial melting of this same plume head produced a huge pile of flood basalts in northwest India known as the Deccan Traps. All of these volcanic features fall along a southwest-northeast-trending line in the Indian Ocean.

The Hawaiian Islands are another example of hot spot activity. A hot spot formed this chain of islands in the Pacific Ocean after it formed Midway Island to the northwest and the Emperor Seamount Chain before that even farther northwest. The flood basalts initially associated with this hot spot have no doubt disappeared through subduction down the trench off the Kuril Islands northeast of Japan. In the United States, the Yellowstone hot spot marks the most recent volcanic activity related to a chain of volcanic centers that traces a line back across the Snake River Plain volcanic province in Idaho and into Washington. Geologists identify mantle plumes related to hot spots almost exclusively by the intraplate volcanism associated with them because, to date, geologists have not been able to detect plumes by geophysical investigation.

SUBDUCTION: PARTIAL MELTING DUE TO THE ADDITION OF WATER

Lithospheric plates that are subducted are relatively cold, dense, and rigid, and comprise the oceanic crust and the lithospheric mantle down to a depth of about 60 miles (100 kilometers). When the oceanic lithosphere is created at a mid-ocean ridge, its upper crust comes into contact with circulating hot seawater, often for millions of years. This produces water-bearing minerals such as micas, amphiboles, clays, and serpentine in the original crustal rock. Carried down by relatively higher density, these lithospheric plates penetrate warmer, more-ductile mantle

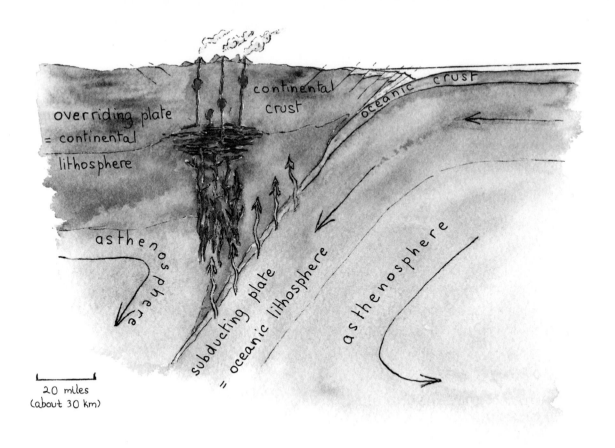

20 miles
(about 30 km)

The supercritical fluid—in which there is no difference between the liquid and vapor phase—migrates up out of the cold slab that is being subducted and into a wedge of overlying, hotter mantle.

material at rates of up to about 4 inches (10 centimeters) per year. Parallel to the zone of subduction, which is generally marked on the surface by an oceanic trench, a chain of volcanoes forms: island arcs in oceanic areas or chains of andesitic volcanoes (named for the Andes in South America) on continents. Andesitic volcanoes erupt lavas that harden into the igneous rock andesite, which has a larger percentage of silica than basalt. This great number of large volcanoes testifies to the production of great quantities of magma related to subduction. So how are these magmas produced?

Owing to the poor thermal conductivity of rocks, the lithospheric slab that is being subducted heats very slowly as it plunges down into the asthenosphere. As a result its temperature remains low, even as the pressure increases with depth. Normally the rocks in the slab would never reach their point of partial melting due to the low temperature; therefore subducted slabs generally are not the direct source of the basaltic magmas that erupt to form island arcs or chains of andesitic volcanoes. However, the water-bearing minerals that are present become unstable at high pressures, and they are transformed into other minerals that contain much less water or are anhydrous (water free) altogether, producing a supercritical fluid. At this point, because of the pressure and temperature conditions, there is no longer any difference between the liquid and vapor phase of the fluid. Due to its much lower density than the surrounding minerals, the freed water migrates up out of the cold slab that is being subducted and into a wedge of overlying, hotter mantle known as a *mantle wedge*. The addition of water to this hot mantle considerably lowers the melting point of its rock, giving rise to large volumes of magma that are very water rich. These magmas feed the violently explosive volcanoes that develop above subduction zones.

MAGMA POOLING: PARTIAL MELTING DUE TO INCREASED TEMPERATURE

Once partial melts have been extracted from mantle peridotites, they rise toward the surface. However, there are often many barriers for the magmas to overcome on their way to the surface and before they can erupt as lavas. One substantial barrier is the boundary between the continental crust and the mantle. The rock at the base of the crust is much less dense than basalt, and it also behaves in a ductile manner, so it does not fracture easily and offer passage to rising magma as does the crustal rock closer to the earth's surface in the brittle zone. However, this rock melts at relatively low temperatures, around 1,500 degrees

Fahrenheit (about 800 degrees Celsius), so when a body of magma at roughly 2,400 degrees Fahrenheit (about 1,300 degrees Celsius) arrives and ponds beneath the crust, there is a significant transfer of heat from magma to crust. This results in partial, or even total, melting of the bounding crustal rock, and this new melt is granitic in composition—called *rhyolitic magma*. These magmas have a high proportion of silica. When rhyolitic magmas reach the surface, they form highly explosive volcanoes that are characterized by large-scale ignimbrites and often caldera collapse.

The only recent case of a rhyolitic eruption was in Alaska in 1912, where the Novarupta Volcano of the Katmai area erupted violently but secretly, as nobody had the opportunity to watch this event. This eruption filled the Valley of Ten Thousand Smokes with ignimbrite. About 600,000 years ago, the emplacement of deep basaltic magma chambers beneath the northern United States resulted in the melting of a large quantity of overlying continental crust, giving rise to the Yellowstone ignimbrite province in Wyoming.

VOLCANIC ROCK DIVERSITY

Volcanic rocks are very diverse, both in texture (size and arrangement of crystals) and color. Texture is determined by the cooling conditions of a particular magma, whereas the color, from the deepest gray to brightest white, reflects the wide range of mineral and chemical compositions found in volcanic rocks.

COOLING HISTORY

Practically all lavas that erupt at the surface of the earth are composed of silicate liquid with randomly distributed atoms, ions, and ion groups. Depending on a fairly different proportion of silica in the liquid, geologists recognize two main magma types: basaltic and rhyolitic, which cool to form low-silica basalt and high-silica rhyolite, respectively.

Following eruption, the temperature of a lava drops at rather constant pressure, and crystals begin to form as the lava hardens. At low temperature, the energy balance makes a rock more stable if the atoms are ordered in regular structures such as crystal lattices. However, for crystals to form, the atoms and ions need to be mobile within the melt, so the viscosity of the lava, which is largely a function of its chemical composition and temperature, is a very important factor.

As a low-silica lava (for example, basaltic) cools at a relatively high temperature (1,800 to 1,500 degrees Fahrenheit; about 1,000 to 800 degrees Celsius), it has a low viscosity—the lava is rather fluid. Under these conditions, the mobility of individual atoms and ions is sufficient to form well-crystallized rocks. On the other hand, high-silica lavas (for example, rhyolitic) that cool at lower temperatures (1,500 to 1,100 degrees Fahrenheit; about 800 to 600 degrees Celsius) are much more viscous—the lavas are pasty. Under these conditions, the atoms and ions are less mobile, which impedes crystallization to the point where it may be impossible.

If a lava cools very rapidly, its viscosity increases abruptly and the lava quenches, forming glass, which doesn't have a crystalline structure. Despite being hard and breakable, window glass is not an ordered solid: it is not crystalline and is, instead, a quenched liquid.

Obsidian

Natural volcanic glass is called *obsidian*. It can form when basaltic lava is quenched, or when silica-rich lava (rhyolitic) cools rapidly. In the first case, the quenching occurs when the hot magma comes into contact with cold seawater or lake water. The lava is chilled to such a degree that all movement of atoms is suppressed and the lava solidifies to form glass, keeping its structural disorder. Basaltic obsidian is often found in the rims of pillow lavas that form at mid-ocean ridges, and also where lava flows reach the sea, such as on the island of Hawai'i or Réunion Island near Madagascar. Underwater eruptions can also form hyaloclastites, a deposit that contains tiny fragments of quenched glass that form when lava shatters upon contact with cool water. Eruptions on dry land can also produce natural glass. When lava erupts as droplets or very thin threads, it cools quickly. The threads of glass are called *Pelé's hair*. Basaltic obsidian flows are very rare on land; one notable occurrence is in the Azrou region of the Middle Atlas Mountains in Morocco.

Silica-rich lavas are usually very viscous when they erupt at the surface, so even with slow cooling it is difficult for crystals to form. The resulting obsidian is a black glass with white patches of pumice, which is also a glass, where bubbles of gas were trapped in the magma when it degassed. Crystals in silica-rich lavas are rare or absent. Small, curved fractures, which develop as the lava continues to cool after solidification, frequently give these rocks what is called a *perlitic* structure. This structure is characterized by tiny beadlike features up to 1/8 inch (3 millimeters) in diameter. Very homogeneous obsidian flows, such as at Lipari in the Lipari Islands near Sicily, or the island of Mílos in the Aegean Sea, were extensively exploited by Paleolithic and Neolithic peoples for the production of cutting tools, which they exported throughout the Mediterranean region.

Microlitic and Doleritic Textures

Lavas that are neither too rich in silica (basaltic or andesitic) nor subject to quenching have time to partially or fully crystallize as they cool from their temperature of eruption, up to 2,200 degrees Fahrenheit (about 1,200 degrees Celsius), to about 900 degrees Fahrenheit (about 500 degrees Celsius), the temperature at which the atoms are no longer mobile enough to form crystals. Microlites, a class of small, lath-shaped

When lava erupts as droplets or very thin threads, it cools quickly. The hardened threads of glass are called Pelé's hair.

Microlitic texture

1/8 inch (3mm)

Doleritic texture

crystals a few tenths of a millimeter long, form in a fine crystalline or glassy matrix under these conditions. Igneous rocks with this arrangement of crystals are said to have a *microlitic texture*. At the time of crystallization, lava is often still fluid enough to flow, so microlites will align with the direction of the lava's movement, creating a microlitic flow texture.

If a lava cools slowly, the microlites grow larger at the expense of the matrix, which may disappear completely. The igneous rock ends up with larger interlocking crystals that enclose smaller, irregular areas where well-formed crystals could not develop. This is called *doleritic texture*. Dikes intruded into basement rocks tend to cool relatively slowly, and they often develop a doleritic texture. A single, thick lava flow may exhibit microlitic texture along its margins, where cooling was more rapid, and a gradual increase in crystal size toward the center of the flow, producing a doleritic texture.

Aphyric versus Porphyritic Texture

Many lavas are very fine grained, in which the largest crystals are tiny microlites. Other lavas contain large, sometimes very abundant, well-formed crystals termed *phenocrysts*, up to 1 inch (about 3 centimeters) in size. Rocks containing phenocrysts have a porphyritic texture. All art lovers know of the green antique porphyry, a volcanic rock containing large phenocrysts, from which the Greeks and Romans carved a number of ornamental vessels and statues. Rocks without phenocrysts are called *aphyric*. Both microlitic and doleritic lavas can be aphyric or porphyritic depending on the conditions in which they formed.

1/8 inch (3mm)

Rocks containing phenocrysts have a porphyritic texture.

The presence of phenocrysts in a rock reveals something about the history of its magma, namely that it must have resided in a magma chamber for some time (up to several tens of years) before erupting, giving the crystals a chance to grow large in slow cooling conditions. The type and chemical composition of the phenocrysts can provide information about the temperature and pressure of a particular magma chamber, allowing volcanologists to estimate the depth of the magma chamber. This information is very useful when studying an active volcano, helping volcanologists understand how the system works, and helping them to try to predict future activity. One consequence of crystallization in the magma chamber is that the composition of the remaining magma evolves, which is one of the reasons why lavas—even if they come from the same source—can be so chemically diverse.

CHEMICAL DIVERSITY

Over the last two centuries, geologists and volcanologists have identified a huge number of volcanic rocks based on their mineralogy and chemistry. Because mineralogy and chemistry varies so widely to begin with, there has been a tendency to assign each different rock a new name, leading to a nomenclature of igneous rocks that is very convoluted. A number of scientists have tried to bring order to the chaos, presenting various classification schemes. However, none of them is completely satisfactory. Even today, although we know much about the formation and evolution of magmas, and it is possible to organize families of lavas within coherent groups, the number of rock types is still very great, and to be able to identify the petrological makeup of igneous rocks requires much practice. So why is there so much diversity? There are several reasons.

Differences in Source Material and Degree of Partial Melting

Magma originates through partial melting of the mantle and continental crust. Both are very rich in oxygen (more than 40 percent of total mass), but they are otherwise very different chemically. The mantle is ultramafic: it is silica poor (silica, or silicon oxide, is less than 40 percent of total mass) and magnesium rich (magnesium oxide is 40 percent of total mass). The continental crust is essentially granitic in composition, meaning it is silica rich (65 to 70 percent of total mass) and aluminum rich (aluminum oxide is about 14 percent of total mass). Partial melts derived from these two sources are thus completely different from each other. The mantle supplies magmas that form dark-colored basalts, which are low in silica but rich in iron and magnesium. The majority of eruptions on the earth today are of basaltic magmas. The continental crust melts to give magmas that form light-colored rhyolites and are silica and aluminum rich. The composition of these two magma types is not constant, as the mantle and crust can be locally heterogeneous, producing different melt compositions during partial melting.

The principal cause of the chemical diversity of magmas, however, is variability in the degree of partial melting—in other words, the amount of melt extracted from a particular mass of rock. A very low degree of melting (up to 5 percent of total mass) in the mantle produces alkali basalts. These basalts are associated with waning hot spot activity, or more usually with continental rift volcanism—as in the East African Rift Valley, the Massif Central region of France, or the San Carlos area in Arizona—where tectonic movement was or is stretching a continent. These silica-poor magmas are rich in strongly incompatible elements, such as sodium and potassium, which enter a mantle melt at the onset of partial melting. As the degree of melting increases (up to around 20 percent of total mass), the silica content of the melt increases, resulting in a basaltic magma that forms a rock called *olivine tholeiite*. Olivine tholeiites are typical of mid-ocean ridge basalts, as well as island arc and continental arc volcanoes. An even higher degree of melting (more than 30 percent of total mass) produces the basalt known as *quartz tholeiite*. This basalt is common in flood basalt provinces and is the result of large-scale melting in a plume head.

Prior to 540 million years ago, in Precambrian time, even higher degrees of melting (more than 40 percent of total mass) occurred, leading to the production of magnesium-rich lavas called *komatiites*.

Magma Mixing and Contamination
Bimodal Volcanism

The emplacement of large basaltic magma chambers in the continental crust often raises the temperature of the surrounding rock high enough to partially or wholly melt it. This causes two contrasting magma types to develop, which erupt at the surface: dark basalts directly from the magma chamber, and light rhyolites or rhyodacites from the partial melting of the crust. In cases like this—when the two magmas don't mix—there are no rocks of intermediate composition, and geologists call these contrasting volcanic assemblages *bimodal*.

Magma Mixing or Hybridization

In certain situations, for example when major tectonic movements accompany the emplacement of basaltic magma, mixing can occur between basaltic magma and melts generated from the surrounding crust.

Tectonic movements and thermal convection may mechanically mix the two magmas. The composition of the rocks erupted at the surface is a reflection of the relative proportions of basaltic and rhyolitic magmas that were in the chamber. For example, Oregon's High Lava Plains exhibit a set of intermediate lava compositions that range between basalt and rhyolite, namely andesite, dacite, and rhyodacite.

Due to the contrast in viscosity between the highly fluid basaltic magma and the more-viscous rhyolitic magma, mixing is not always complete. Inhomogeneities in volcanic rock occur on many scales—from microscopic to entire lava flows—with lighter and darker portions reflecting incomplete mixing. Another indication that magma mixing occurred is a sharp change in the composition of phenocrysts, which began to crystallize in a melt of a particular composition, and then continued to grow in a mixed magma that had a different composition. The result is compositionally zoned phenocrysts. The zoning reflects the chemical changes that occurred during crystallization.

Contamination

Smaller basaltic magma chambers cannot heat surrounding continental crust enough to melt it. However, blocks of crust that are torn off the chamber walls can contaminate the magma. These blocks are more or less melted in the hot, 2,200-degree-Fahrenheit (1,200-degree-Celsius) magma and are assimilated in the basalt, producing intermediate lava compositions. In this case, lavas of a strictly crustal composition are not observed. The final magma, however, may be heterogeneous due to incomplete assimilation of the blocks, and the cooled volcanic rock can contain a number of xenoliths—pieces of the crust that were extracted by the magma but did not melt.

Magmatic Differentiation by Fractional Crystallization

Magma crystallizes progressively during cooling as long as the temperature is high enough to prevent it from solidifying to a glass. Unlike crystals that form in water or sugar syrup (ice or sugar crystals respectively), which have the same composition as the host liquid, crystals growing early on in magma have a very different composition from their host magma. For example, one of the first crystals to form from a basaltic magma is olivine, which has a chemical composition of magnesium-rich silicate. As olivine crystallizes, the remaining magma becomes magnesium impoverished but enriched in many other elements that are not found in the olivine crystals, such as sodium, calcium, and aluminum, or are found in small amounts, such as iron. The same effect will happen when the crystallization of another mineral, for example, clinopyroxene, occurs in the magma after olivine crystallization. This effect is known as *fractional crystallization*, and the resulting evolution of the magma is called *magmatic differentiation*. Imagine a magma chamber experiencing magmatic differentiation: if batches of magma are somehow periodically squeezed out to the earth's surface, each eruption would have a slightly different composition compared to the previous one.

Another way to think about fractional crystallization is to remember that compatible elements prefer to enter into a crystal structure rather than remain in a disordered melt, leaving the incompatible elements concentrated in the magma. The minerals that form first, such as chromite, olivine, augite, and hornblende, preferentially incorporate chromium instead of aluminum, magnesium instead of iron, and calcium instead of sodium. At the same time, incompatible elements are concentrated in the liquid that remains in between the crystals. If crystallization continues, new minerals such as plagioclase, sanidine, nepheline, or cristobalite form in that interstitial liquid, which has a composition that is very different from that of the initial magma. Thus the quantity of liquid decreases as crystallization progresses, and the composition of the remaining melt is continuously modified.

Once the magma erupts at the surface, it is only a matter of a few minutes to a few days—at most a few months—before the lava is completely solid. Most crystals that form after an eruption are tiny microlites, and the lava, taken as a solidified whole, directly reflects the composition of the erupted magma. Because of fractional crystallization, a magma of a given composition can create many different derivative igneous rock types.

Crystallization in a Magma Chamber

Cooling and crystallization in a magma chamber takes place at a much slower rate, on the order of years to centuries. The crystals have time to become large, and they often occur as phenocrysts in cooled lavas after a magma chamber erupts. In most cases, phenocrysts have a greater density relative to magma, and along with their large size, they have a tendency to sink ¾ inch to 10 feet (2 centimeters to 3 meters) per day and accumulate at the bottom of a chamber. The phenocrysts build up layers of granular rocks called *cumulates*. Cumulates may also form on the sides of a chamber, where cooling is more rapid. As these crystals settle out, they take with them the compatible elements of the melt. The remaining magma becomes progressively enriched in incompatible elements—silica, aluminum, sodium, and potassium—as long as fractional crystallization proceeds. This chemical evolution, resulting from fractional crystallization as the magma cools, is called *magmatic differentiation*.

Eruption of magma from a chamber can occur at any stage of magmatic differentiation, feeding volcanoes with lavas of various compositions. A differentiated melt coming from a deep reservoir may, in turn, be stored in a shallower magma chamber. It can then experience a second stage of fractional crystallization, producing increasingly differentiated melts. The genetic relationship between the different members of such a lava series can be revealed by inclusions of cumulate material, which are torn from the chamber walls and brought to the surface by erupting magma.

A good example of this process of magmatic differentiation is exhibited in the volcanic rocks of the Chaîne des Puys volcanic province

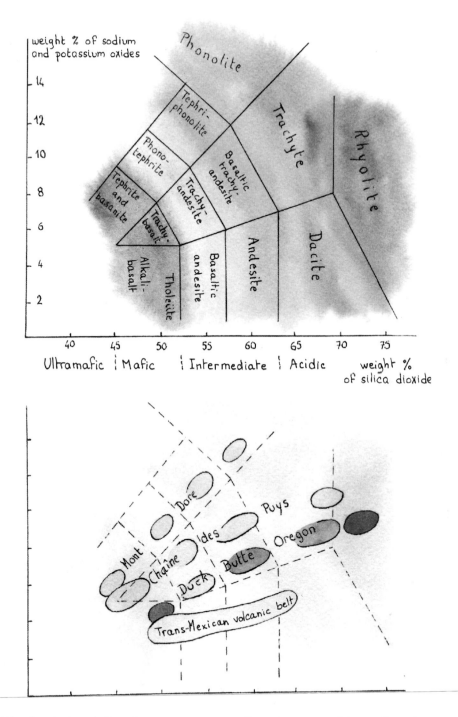

The chemical evolution of a magma can occur through magma mixing or through magmatic differentiation as the magma cools in a chamber, or both. Both processes produce similar volcanic rocks at the surface. For example, although they show very similar patterns, the Chaîne des Puys volcanic series is almost exclusively related to fractional crystallization, while the Duck Butte series of Oregon is related almost exclusively to magma mixing. Conversely, although showing fairly different differentiation patterns, both the Mont-Dore series in France and the Trans-Mexican volcanic belt series of Mexico result from mixing of basaltic and crustal magmas.

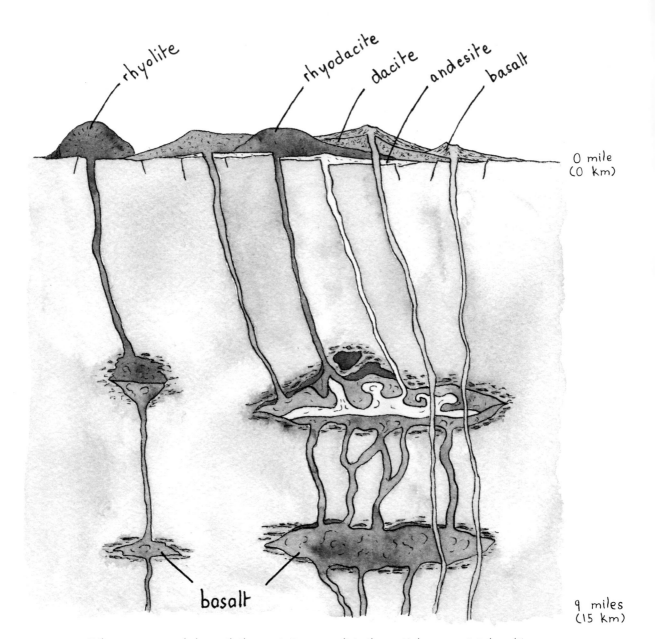

When magma pools beneath the crust, it can result in the partial, or even total, melting of the bounding crustal rocks, leading to a rhyolitic magma erupted at the surface. When tectonic movements or thermal convection mix basaltic and rhyolitic magmas, the composition of the intermediate lava erupted at the surface is a reflection of the relative proportions of the basaltic and rhyolitic magmas that were in the chamber to begin with.

in France. Here the lavas show a chemical progression from low-silica basalt to silica-rich trachyte, with intermediate trachybasalts, trachyandesites, and basaltic trachyandesites. Studies of the lavas indicate that this continuous compositional series was caused by the fractionation of olivine, augite, and amphibole in deep magma chambers, forming the basaltic to trachyandesitic rocks, followed by fractionation of amphibole and plagioclase at shallower levels, which produced the trachytes. In the Mont-Dore Massif in France, one of the two identified magmatic series exhibits a range from low-silica basanite to high-silica phonolite with intermediate-silica tephritic compositions.

Unraveling a Lava's History

There are two basic mechanisms for producing the chemical diversity seen in volcanic rock: magmatic differentiation, caused by fractional crystallization, and the mixing of basaltic magma and crustal rock through hybridization or contamination. Both mechanisms result in very similar magmatic series of erupted rocks characterized by a progressive evolution from basaltic to rhyolitic rocks erupted at the surface. Sometimes both mechanisms play a role in a single magma series; for example, if cumulates and xenoliths both are present in a hardened lava. So how is it possible to distinguish which mechanism prevailed when trying to unravel the magmatic history of a volcanic zone? The answer often lies in the detailed study of rock chemistry. Volcanologists investigate the behavior of trace elements and isotopes of certain elements.

Trace Elements

In addition to major elements such as silicon, aluminum, iron, magnesium, and calcium, volcanic rocks also contain numerous trace elements, which are rare and often occur in quantities measured in parts per million or parts per billion. Like major elements, trace elements occur as ions in magma, and the size of each one is regarded as its ionic radius. Smaller ions, such as nickel, chromium, and cobalt,

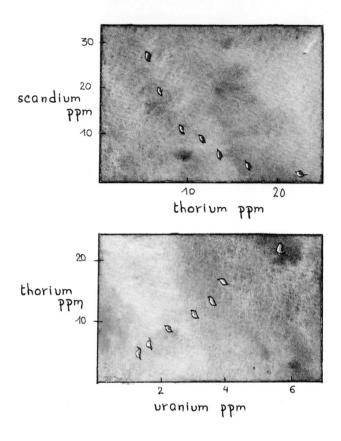

Deviations from these model trends indicate to volcanologists that fractional crystallization was not the only mechanism involved in the evolution of a magmatic series.

are compatible, and they enter easily into crystal structures even at high temperatures in a melt. These elements are rapidly removed from a magma at the earliest stages of cooling and crystallization. Larger ions, such as uranium and thorium, are magmaphiles, or incompatible elements, and they tend to concentrate in a magma as it cools during crystallization. Most trace elements behave in a manner that is somewhere in between these two extremes. Because ions in magma behave in predictable ways, geologists can unravel the magmatic history of a volcanic series by comparing the concentrations of major and trace elements of all individual rock types.

When fractional crystallization was the dominant mechanism in the evolution of a magmatic series, the chemical composition of its lava follows a predictable pattern in terms of the concentration of major and trace elements. In a simple graph, where the concentrations of two incompatible elements are plotted against one another, the result is a linear (straight-line) relationship. For example, when thorium is plotted against uranium, both elements increase in abundance in a magma as it progressively crystallizes. On the other hand, when the concentration of a compatible element, like scandium, is plotted against an incompatible element, like thorium, the result is a hyperbolic curve. As a magma cools and crystallizes, there is a drop in the abundance of scandium as the concentration of thorium increases. Deviations from these model trends indicate to volcanologists that fractional crystallization was not the only mechanism involved in the evolution of a particular magmatic series.

Isotopic Ratios

An atom is composed of protons (which have positive electrical charges), neutrons (which are neutral electrically), and electrons (which have negative electrical charges and balance the protons). Each element has an atomic number, which is the number of protons a single atom of that element has in its nucleus. For example, strontium's atomic number is 38. The sum of the number of an atom's neutrons and protons is its mass number. All atoms of a given element have the same atomic number, but the number of neutrons in a given atom—which affects the atom's mass—can vary. These different forms of the same element are called isotopes. All isotopes of a given element have the same chemical properties, but geologists can separate them in a rock sample using a mass spectrometer. This machine accelerates isotopes into a magnetic field, where they are separated according to their mass. Geologists then calculate the ratios of certain isotopes in a given sample and compare them.

The element strontium exists as four natural isotopes: strontium-84, strontium-86, strontium-87, and strontium-88. Neodymium has seven natural isotopes, of which the main ones are neodymium-142, neodymium-143, neodymium-144, and neodymium-146. The numbers denote

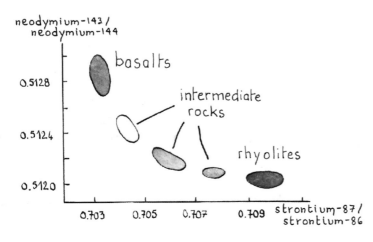

Geologists use isotopic ratios to assess the relative contribution of the crust and mantle in a differentiated series of lavas.

the isotope's mass. The isotopes of these two elements are important to geologists when trying to date volcanic rock and determine its magmatic evolution. The proportions of these isotopes in a rock may shift over time, because certain isotopes are radioactive. A radioactive isotope is one that emits radiation and in doing so decays to a different radiogenic daughter element. For each radioactive isotope, this process of radioactive decay occurs at a known rate, which is called its *decay rate*.

For example, rubidium-87 decays to strontium-87, and the isotope samarium-147 decays to neodymium-143. As a result, the samarium-neodymium and rubidium-strontium isotopic compositions of an igneous rock change with time. A mass spectrometer allows geologists to measure isotopic ratios, so they typically measure the ratio of a radioactive or radiogenic isotope (one that grows with time) to an isotope of the same element that does not change with time (one that is neither radiogenic nor radioactive). The isotopic ratios of strontium-87 (radiogenic) to strontium-86 (constant) and neodymium-143 (radiogenic) to neodymium-144 (constant) will change with time, with the rate of change dependant on how much rubidium and samarium the rock originally contained and how long the radioactive rubidium and samarium have been decaying into strontium-87 and neodymium-143. Geologists use this temporal information to estimate the age of igneous rocks in a field of research called *geochronology*.

Isotopes are also extremely useful for distinguishing between the different mechanisms of chemical evolution in a magma series. Since isotopes of a single element have identical chemical properties, they behave the same during partial melting and fractional crystallization. Thus all magmas from a differentiated series will start with the same isotopic ratios in a hardened rock that they had at the time of their differentiation in a magma chamber. These ratios slowly change with time, and the changes are dependant on the initial concentrations of elements like rubidium-87 and samarium-147 in a particular magma. Conversely, when two magmas were mixed in a magma chamber, the isotopes of the mixed magma faithfully reflect the isotopic concentrations of the two original magmas. This is particularly clear when crustal melts are involved because crustal melts have very different isotopic ratios compared to magmas derived from the mantle. So by comparing the ratios of certain isotopes in a particular magma, geologists can determine whether or not mixing occurred in the magma chamber and even have a fairly accurate estimate of the proportion of each of the initial components in the resulting igneous rock.

DATING VOLCANIC EVENTS

In order to understand how a volcano, or a volcanic region, has behaved over a long period of time, geologists need to know the chronology of eruptions. There are several methods for gathering this information.

HISTORY

Major volcanic events were registered in ancient texts, particularly eruptions that occurred adjacent to the Greek, Roman, and Japanese civilizations. The first mention of an eruption of Mount Etna was part of the history of the emigration of the Sicanes people in 1400 BC, which was written by Didor of Sicily. Since he wrote the book over thirteen centuries after the emigration, it is unclear what his information was based on and how accurate it was. Further eruptions of Mount Etna were recorded from the fifth century BC onward by Thucydides, Plato, Virgil, St. Augustine, Strabo, Suetonius, and others. It has only been since the seventeenth century that modern historians have compiled a complete record of this mountain's volcanic activity. Vesuvius, in Italy, has also been well documented since Roman times, most notably by Pliny the Elder and Pliny the Younger. However, the majority of volcanic eruptions occurred away from civilizations with a written tradition, and their record was instead preserved orally—often very vividly and much appreciated by ethnologists. This orally recorded information lacks the precision to be of much practical use to volcanologists, but they can use the information to create a general chronology of events for a volcano or volcanic region.

RELATIVE CHRONOLOGY

By deciphering the structure of a volcano, volcanologists can determine the sequence of eruptive events in the volcano's history. Assessing the relative age of rock units is based upon certain simple principles of geological mapping: the principle of superposition, in which the oldest layer of rock lies at the bottom and the youngest at the top of a cross section of rocks; the principle of juxtaposition, in which the youngest

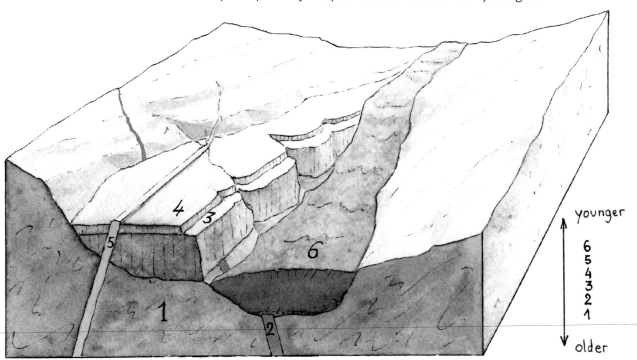

The principles of superposition, juxtaposition, and crosscutting relations help geologists determine the relative chronology of a volcano's rocks and eruptive events.

lava flows may be topographically lower than the oldest, and therefore superficially defy the principle of superposition; and the principle of crosscutting relations, in which a rock that cuts across another must be the younger of the two. These rules are very difficult to apply to volcanoes that have had a long history with multiple phases of construction, repose, and destruction. In addition, the fieldwork necessary to observe relations between eruptive units is often hampered by snow, ice, or dense vegetation that conceals the rock outcrops. For example, a lava flow that formed in 1977 on Réunion Island was almost completely obscured by 2002.

Despite the difficulties and limitations inherent in volcanic mapping, it still remains an essential part of understanding a volcano and its eruptive style and history. It is good, though, to be able to calibrate this relative chronology with actual dates for some of the eruptive deposits.

ABSOLUTE CHRONOLOGY

Absolute dating yields an age for an eruptive event, be it years ago or millions of years ago. The term "absolute" is a little misleading since all age determinations have a certain amount of error associated with the measurement, which can sometimes be quite significant. In fact, measured ages may appear to contradict the principle of superposition if a margin of error is not taken into account. Geologists commonly use three methods to obtain absolute dates from volcanic rocks: carbon-14 dating, potassium-argon dating, and thermoluminescence.

Carbon-14 Dating

The carbon-14 dating method is based on the concentration of the isotope carbon-14 in organic material, or by measuring the ratio of carbon-14 and carbon-12 concentrations in organic material—carbon-12 being the stable and more-abundant isotope. Carbon-14 is called a *cosmogenic isotope* since it continuously forms in the upper atmosphere as the nitrogen isotope nitrogen-14 is bombarded by cosmic rays. Carbon-14 is radioactive and decays back to nitrogen-14. The half-life for this transformation is 5,730 years—at the end of this length of time exactly half of a given quantity of carbon-14 will have decayed. Broadly speaking, the production and decay of carbon-14 in the atmosphere is balanced, so the carbon in atmospheric carbon dioxide has a carbon-14–carbon-12 ratio that has stayed relatively constant for the last 100,000 years. Organisms that interact with the atmosphere, particularly plants, which incorporate carbon dioxide during photosynthesis, have a balanced carbon-14–carbon-12 ratio while they are living.

When a lava flow destroys a wooded area, the trees are carbonized. Once dead, they are no longer equilibrated with the atmosphere since they no longer take up carbon dioxide. The concentration of carbon-14 in the carbonized wood decays to nitrogen-14 following the well-known decay rate. Geologists can determine the age of a lava flow by measuring the concentration of carbon-14 in the carbonized wood, either by measuring the beta radioactivity of a pure carbon sample with a known weight, or by mass spectrometry.

This dating method is widely used in volcanology, and archaeologists use it to date prehistoric fireplaces. Since carbon-14 has such a short half-life, this method can only be used on material up to 100,000 years old; beyond that there is too little carbon-14 present to be detectable. Another constraint is that carbonized organic material must be present in the volcanic deposits being studied, which is not always the case.

Potassium-Argon Dating

The potassium-argon dating method is a widely applicable dating method since all igneous rocks contain potassium, a tiny portion of which is the radioactive isotope potassium-40. This isotope produces argon-40 through a complex decay sequence. The half-life for this process is 1.25 billion years.

Because argon is a gas, argon-40 only begins to build up in rocks and minerals after they have fully solidified. Geologists measure argon-40 in a sample using mass spectrometry, and then deduce the original concentration of potassium-40 by measuring the total amount of potassium in a rock or crystal. The absolute age of a sample since solidification, then, is proportional to the quantity of argon-40 in the sample. Any loss or addition of argon subsequent to crystallization will result in an erroneous date. Since potassium-40 has such a long half-life, there is no upper age limit for dating rocks using this method. Conversely, due to limited accuracy, the method is only suitable for dating rocks 1 million years old or older, unless special analytical devices are employed.

During the last two decades, the potassium-argon method has been superseded by another method that employs two argon isotopes: argon-39 and argon-40. This method is much more precise, but it is more complicated to perform since the sample has to be irradiated in a nuclear reactor prior to being analyzed. It is suitable for dating rocks that are 30,000 years old or older.

Another method that geologists increasingly are using is based on measuring isotopic disequilibrium between uranium and its decay products, notably thorium. Geologists can date samples with ages lying between the present and 350,000 years ago using this technique, thus filling the gap between the carbon-14 and argon-39–argon-40 techniques. However, this method is a bit too difficult to explain in this book.

Thermoluminescence

Certain minerals produce a one-time weak flash of light when they are heated. This is called *natural thermoluminescence*. Using artificial irradiation in a nuclear reactor, scientists have shown that radiation triggers certain atoms in crystals to be excited—meaning the atoms' electrons are bumped up to higher energy levels. Subsequent heating allows these excited electrons to return to their initial state, releasing energy in the form of photons, or light. The amount of light emitted is proportional to the intensity of the radiation the atoms were exposed to and the duration of exposure.

The same phenomenon happens in some minerals (fluorite, calcite, quartz, feldspar) that compose various rocks. Some atoms are excited when exposed to natural radioactive decay, and excited electrons are trapped in some atoms of the crystal lattice. The age of one of these minerals can be determined by measuring the intensity of radioactivity in the rock surrounding it along with the amount of light the sample emits when heated—the older the rock, the more light the mineral emits. Volcanologists and archaeologists have used this method to date rocks or artifacts that are from a few years to around 1 million years old. Geologists have dated many eruptions in the Chaîne des Puys volcanic province in France, from 6,000 to 100,000 years old, measuring the thermoluminescence of quartz and feldspar minerals.

PREDICTING VOLCANIC ERUPTIONS

Half a billion people live close to active volcanoes—directly in harm's way of volcanic hazards. The immediate surroundings of these active volcanoes, be they towns or villages, livestock or crops, are continually threatened by partial or complete destruction. For the last one hundred years or so, since eruptive mechanisms have been seriously studied, volcanologists and politicians have tried to safeguard people by developing—and making available—tools to warn local populations of possible eruptions. Eruption forecasting and volcanic risk assessment are not the exclusive purview of fortune-tellers. Instead, they are based on years of patient observation and the careful interpretation of complex volcanic phenomena worldwide.

ESTIMATING THE THREAT

The past is the key to the future. For this reason, volcanologists recognize that having the most complete history possible of a volcanic area is paramount to understanding a volcano and assessing the risk it poses to its surroundings. The study of a dormant volcano, its flows and pyroclastic deposits, is invaluable in the event that volcanic activity starts again. Deposits from lahars, blasts, or nuées ardentes, as well as evidence of zones of collapse on a volcano's flanks, all indicate that potential hazards exist. Volcanologists record relevant information on geological maps and special risk assessment maps, which they use in times of crisis to make quick decisions and to advise officials of an appropriate course of action.

The majority of large, active volcanoes around the world are monitored and studied, though not all to the same level of detail. Smaller volcanoes, or those thought to be safely dormant, do not have risk maps. There are also volcanic hazards that volcanologists cannot predict. For example, a fissure unexpectedly opened up in flat ground—unrelated to any preexisting volcano—and a volcano began forming in Paricutín, Mexico, in 1943.

PRECURSORS OF ERUPTIONS

New volcanic activity, or the reawakening of a dormant volcano, is preceded by signals that provide volcanologists with important information that they can use to predict eruptions.

Seismic Precursors

The ascent of magma from a magma chamber to the surface opens up fissures and fractures beneath a volcanic vent, giving rise to earthquakes, or seismicity. The amplitude of the quakes is usually not very great, but the rapid rise of magma to the surface leads to an increase in the number of these seismic shocks. Thus the onset of intense seismic activity (up to several hundred shocks per hour) is often a precursor to a volcanic eruption. Where a volcano is monitored by a seismic network, either permanent or temporary, the foci of seismic shocks can be pinpointed in three dimensions, and the depth of the foci indicates how imminent an eruption is since the foci tend to coincide with a rising head of magma.

From the time that magma reaches the surface and an eruption begins, there is a permanent connection, or pipe, between a magma chamber and a vent. Ascending magma no longer needs to force a route by fracturing bedrock, so the number of seismic shocks decreases considerably. However, the magma and gas transfer through the pipe give rise to low-frequency vibrations known as *tremors*. These generally begin to be registered, and increase in intensity, just before an eruption. Tremor intensity culminates with the eruptive paroxysm, and volcanologists consider its decline as an indication that the eruption has ended.

Inflation of Volcanoes

The introduction of a large volume of magma and gas into the region immediately beneath a volcano results in an overall inflation, or expansion, of the volcano. This inflation is small and usually is not visible to the naked eye, but volcanologists can measure it with a variety of instruments.

Tilt Meters

Tilt meters can measure small changes in the angle of volcanic slopes. These instruments contain very sensitive pendulums that are capable of detecting slope differences down to a thousandth of a radian, which is equal to 0.06 of a degree, or 1 inch over 15 miles (1 millimeter per kilometer).

Displacement Meters

Open fissures are common around volcanoes, and they tend to widen during volcano inflation. Volcanologists use displacement meters to precisely measure this enlargement. One part of the instrument, from which a metal pin extends, is fixed to one side of a fissure. The other end of this pin rests inside a cylinder that is fixed to the opposite side of the fissure. This device is sensitive to movements as small as 1 millionth of a millimeter. If the fissure widens, the pin moves within the cylinder, producing an electronic signal. Of course, new fissures can open during inflation, and their very presence is a strong indication that an eruption is imminent.

Electronic Distance Meters

The diameter of a volcano's crater also increases during inflation. Volcanologists measure this distance using an electronic distance meter, which sends laser signals from one side of a crater to reflectors spaced around the crater rim. Volcanologists determine the increase in diameter, measurable to the nearest millimeter, by calculating the time it takes the laser beam to bounce back from the individual reflectors.

Spatial Altimetry

Satellites orbiting the earth can also provide volcanologists with information on volcanic inflation. Using the Global Positioning System (receivers are set up on the flanks of volcanoes), volcanologists can detect relative movements, lateral or vertical, down to around a millimeter by comparing data provided by several adjacent Global Positioning System receivers.

Another satellite-based technique involves comparing radar images taken at regular time intervals by satellites. Volcanologists can detect minute changes in a volcano's altitude by superimposing successive images. The precision of this method is on the order of $\frac{3}{8}$ inch (I centimeter) over an area of about 4,000 square miles

Volcanologists can measure the amount a volcano's diameter expands when the volcano inflates using an electronic distance meter.

(10,000 square kilometers), which makes this approach useful for the surveillance of entire volcanic systems.

The drawback to satellite monitoring is that it is sensitive to weather conditions. Changes in air temperature, in particular, affect the velocity of the electromagnetic waves that satellites emit and receive.

Thermal and Chemical Precursors

The rise of magma into shallow chambers, and eventually to the surface, brings a great amount of heat to a volcanic structure. Before an eruption takes place, this heat produces a noticeable increase in the temperature of groundwater that may circulate convectively within and near a volcano. The introduction of hot, magmatic fluids into a hydrothermal system can also cause temperature increases. If fumaroles are present, their temperatures rise abruptly, as do the temperatures of natural springs on the flanks of a volcano or in crater lakes. A significant influx of magmatic fluid also modifies water composition. By monitoring the temperature and composition of hydrothermal waters and fumaroles, volcanologists can better understand preeruption magmatic activity at depth.

An influx of magmatic fluids may also accelerate fumarolic activity, and it can be confirmed by measuring the radon output of a fumarole. This radioactive noble gas is produced continuously as uranium in rocks decays. It has a very short half-life (six days), so its presence on the surface of a volcano indicates that the fumarolic gas is moving from depth to the surface very quickly. When the gas transfer is slow, the concentration of radon is generally below the detection limit because most of the radon in the fumarolic gas decayed before reaching the surface. The appearance of new fumaroles is, of course, an important indicator, alerting volcanologists to an imminent eruption.

On a broader scale, volcanologists monitor volcano temperatures by measuring infrared radiation with satellites. Although weather conditions may impact the accuracy of readings because clouds absorb infrared radiation, this method should prove useful to volcanologists.

Magnetic Precursors

Unlike cold, solidified lavas that contain tiny magnetite crystals and behave like natural magnets, hot magmas are not magnetic. A nonmagnetic hot magma body embedded within the magnetic rocks surrounding it can be detected, however, since the magnetic field strength over the hot body will be weaker than normal. Consequently, magma intrusion beneath volcanoes leads to local variations in the strength of the magnetic field, which can be detected with a magnetometer. Tracking these changes helps volcanologists follow the movement of magma at depth.

Fumarolic vapors contain dissolved salts that are deposited along vents in the form of yellow sulfur and white sulfates. By monitoring the temperature and composition of hydrothermal waters and fumaroles, volcanologists can better understand preeruption magmatic activity at depth.

VOLCANO SURVEILLANCE NETWORKS

Volcanologists use the various monitoring techniques described above during an imminent volcanic crisis to attempt to predict the coming eruptive activity. Even after an eruption begins, they continue monitoring in order to forecast an eruption's evolution. Some volcanoes are subject to continuous surveillance, with the information normally being sent by radio to a nearby volcano observatory. This is the case for the three active French volcanoes: le Piton de la Fournaise on Réunion Island off the east coast of Madagascar, Mount Pelée on Martinique Island in the

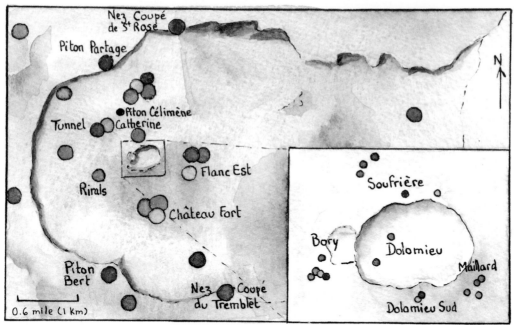

● Electronic distance meter   ○ Magnetometer

● Radon analyser   ● Seismograph

◐ Displacement meter

Le Piton de la Fournaise on Réunion Island is one of the best-monitored volcanoes in the world.

Lesser Antilles, and la Soufrière on Guadeloupe in the Lesser Antilles. Le Piton de la Fournaise is one of the best-monitored volcanoes in the world, with four networks of detectors: seismic, comprising nineteen seismographs; a deformation network, composed of ten tilt meters, four displacement meters, two electronic distance meters with five reflectors, and two Global Positioning System receivers; twenty-two radon detectors; and an eight-station network to monitor magnetic activity. In addition, two stations measure fumarole temperatures. This intensive monitoring has turned Piton de la Fournaise into a field-based laboratory. Kilauea Crater on the island of Hawai'i and Mount St. Helens in Washington are monitored similarly.

Because of this intense monitoring, eruptions of Piton de la Fournaise, which occur frequently but without great risk, are detected in advance. Alarms linked directly to the homes of researchers working at the observatory are triggered with a certain level of seismic activity. La

Soufrière on Guadeloupe, as well as Mount Pelée on Martinique, are not as good-natured as Piton de la Fournaise. Their ancient and more-recent history indicates that both have sporadic but devastating eruptions characterized by Plinian fallout, blasts, and nuées ardentes. The May 1902 eruption of Mount Pelée was the most catastrophic eruption of recent times. Apart from the crisis of 1975–76 at Guadeloupe, and the eruption of Mount Pelée between 1929 and 1932 on Martinique, these

The volcanologists linked to the Chaîne des Puys observatory can sleep happily in peace, knowing that it is unlikely that this extinct volcanic province will erupt again.

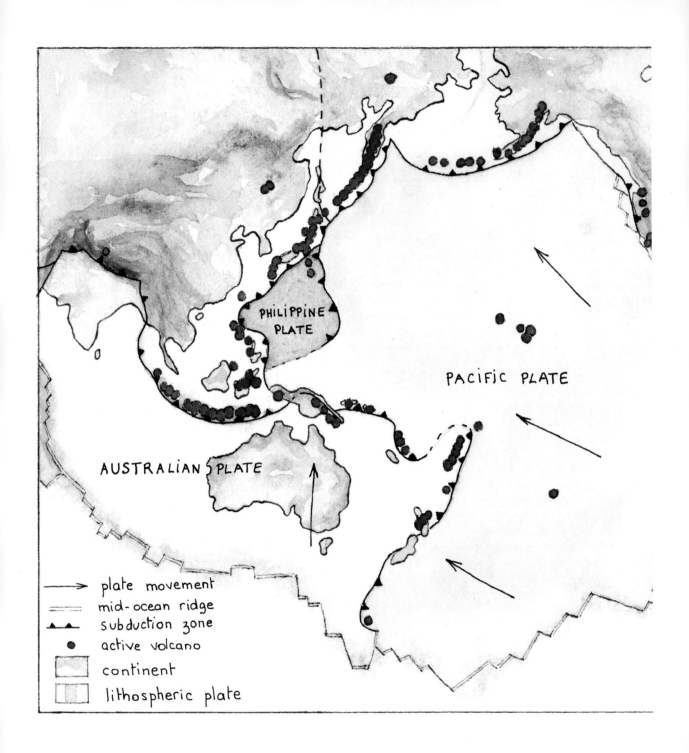

PHILIPPINE PLATE

PACIFIC PLATE

AUSTRALIAN PLATE

→ plate movement
— mid-ocean ridge
▲▲ subduction zone
● active volcano
☐ continent
☐ lithospheric plate

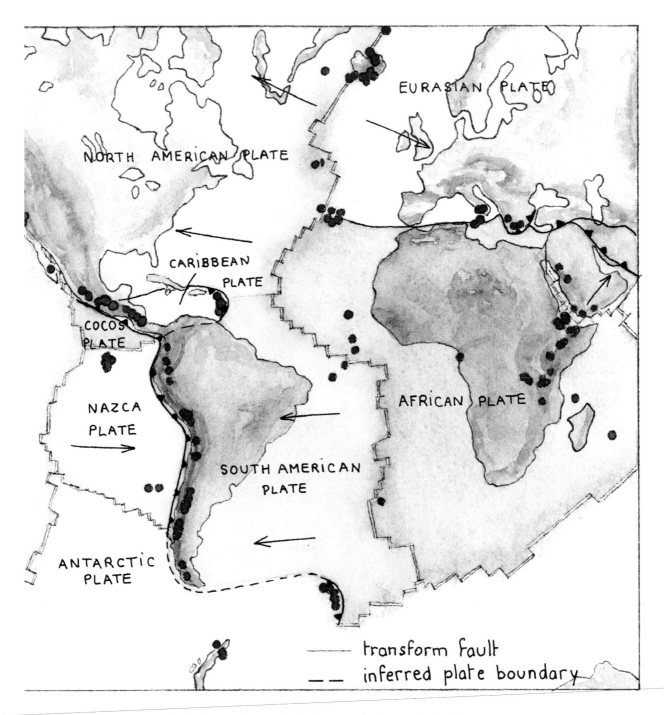

Global map of lithospheric plates and volcano distribution.

two volcanoes have both been relatively quiet for the last century. Nevertheless, they have monitoring networks similar to those found on Piton de la Fournaise, albeit less extensive. Among other detectors, scientists placed a temperature sensor in a drilled hole at a depth of 262 feet (80 meters) on la Soufrière, and Mount Pelée has a geochemical station that simultaneously monitors water level, temperature, electrical conductivity, and the pH (acidity) of water in a well.

As well as these active volcanoes, there are other volcanoes in France and around the world that are extinct, or profoundly dormant. One such example is the Chaîne des Puys volcanic province in central France. The last activity from this region was the explosion of the crater Lac Pavin six thousand years ago. The Puy de Dôme erupted ten thousand years ago. Given the amount of time that has passed since this activity, volcanologists and other decision makers don't feel that it is necessary to have a complex surveillance network in this region. A mere seven seismic stations alone monitor the dormant volcanoes of this large region, and since their installation in 1980 they have not registered any seismic activity of volcanic origin. The volcanologists linked to this observatory can sleep happily in peace, knowing that likely they will never awaken to the alarm of an eruption alert!

GLOSSARY

'a'a. Basaltic lava with a rough surface.

alkali basalt. A silica-poor magma rich in incompatible elements. It is the result of a low degree of partial melting in the mantle.

aphyric. A term that describes the texture of a fine-grained rock that does not have phenocrysts.

ash. Tiny lava fragments, less than $5/64$ inch (2 millimeters) in diameter, that are thrown out by a volcano.

asthenosphere. The plastic and weak region of the upper mantle that deforms easily, allowing a convection cell to develop. It underlies the more rigid lithospheric mantle, starting at a depth of about 60 miles (100 kilometers).

atoms. The building blocks of all matter; they are characterized by differences in their mass and number of electrons.

basalt. A dark, low-silica rock that is the result of partial melting in the mantle.

basement. The complex of rocks that volcanoes develop in and on top of.

black smoker. A chimneylike hydrothermal vent on the seafloor that ejects hot water—over 570°F (300°C)—that turns black due to the precipitation of fine minerals in the hot water.

blast. An explosion with a definite direction, as in a lateral blast.

bomb. A lava fragment measuring more than 2½ inches (64 millimeters) in diameter that is thrown out by a volcano.

caldera. A basin-shaped zone of subsidence that forms after a magma chamber beneath a volcano has emptied.

chamber. *See* magma chamber

chilling. The sudden cooling of hot liquid magma, which freezes atoms in place and prevents further mineral crystallization.

columnar jointing. Elongate, polygonal prisms that form when cooling lava contracts.

compatible. Said of a chemical element that assumes a crystalline form (solid) at a relatively high temperature rather than stay in a magma (liquid).

cone. *See* volcanic cone

contamination. A change in the composition of a magma through the incorporation of material that is broken off the walls and roof of a magma chamber.

continental arc. A chain of volcanoes that develops parallel to a subduction zone.

convection. A mechanism of heat transfer, whereby hot material rises when heated from below and cool material sinks, creating a circulation cell. Convection occurs in the mantle.

core. The central portion of the earth that is composed of a solid, iron-nickel alloy called the *inner core*, which is surrounded by a molten iron and nickel layer called the *outer core*. The inner core has a radius of 758 miles (1,220 kilometers). The outer core lies between the bottom of the mantle, at a depth of 1,796 miles (2,890 kilometers), and the inner core, which starts at a depth of 3,200 miles (5,150 kilometers).

cosmogenic isotope. An isotope that continuosly forms in the atmosphere when a particular element is bombarded by cosmic rays.

crust. The uppermost layer of the earth; generally, it is composed of basalt under oceans and granite under continents.

cryptodome. A viscous lava dome that remains hidden inside an older volcanic cone.

crystal. A natural, inorganic solid with a regularly repeating internal arrangement of atoms and ions. All specimens of a given mineral have the same specific crystal structure.

cumulate. A granular rock composed of phenocrysts that accumulated in a magma chamber.

decay. *See* radioactive decay

decompression. The lowering of the pressure of a solid, liquid, or gas.

differentiation. *See* magmatic defferentiation

dike. A narrow body of intrusive magma that cuts across basement rocks vertically or obliquely.

doleritic. A rock texture characterized by relatively large interlocking microlites.

dome. A steep-sided, dome-shaped body of viscous lava that forms over a fissure or vent, sometimes in the crater of a volcano.

draped lava. A lava flow surface that resembles a draped cloth.

ejecta. *See* volcanic ejecta

fault. A fracture in the earth's crust.

feeder pipe. A tube that supplies magma to a volcano from a magma chamber.

fissure. An elongate crack or opening in rock at the surface from which magma can erupt.

flood basalt. A huge thickness of basaltic lavas erupted over a relatively short period of time (on the order of 1 million years). They are related to former hot spot activity.

flow. An outpouring of lava that covers a volcano's flanks and adjacent valleys.

flow texture. A rock texture in which the microlites or crystals are all more or less parallel. They are aligned with the direction the lava flowed before hardening.

flux. A substance that decreases the melting point of a rock.

fractional crystallization. The separation of crystals from liquid in a magma body—by gravity or crystallization on the wall of a magma chamber—as it cools.

fumarole. The venting of gas on the flanks of, or close to, a volcano.

gabbro. A coarse-grained rock that has crystallized from a basaltic magma.

half-life. The time it takes for half the amount of a radioactive element to decay to a radiogenic daughter element.

hot spot. A point on the earth's surface above a mantle plume. Volcanism associated with hot spots is called *intraplate volcanism*.

hyaloclastite. A submarine deposit composed of glassy rock fragments that formed when lava shattered upon contact with cool water.

hybridization. The chemical evolution of magma due to the mixing of two or more magma types.

hydraulic fracturing. The breakup of solids (for example, brittle crustal rock) due to the pressure transmitted by a liquid body (for example, magma).

ignimbrite. A pyroclastic formation composed of thick layers of pumice and ash.

incompatible. Said of a chemical element that remains in a magma (liquid) at relatively low temperature rather than assuming a crystalline form (solid).

intraplate volcanism. Volcanic activity that does not occur along plate boundaries, but rather at a point (a hot spot) within an oceanic or continental lithospheric plate.

ion. An electrically charged atom—positive or negative.

iron meteorite. A metallic meteorite composed mostly of iron and a lesser amount of nickel. Iron meteorites provide an important clue about the earth's core, which geologists think is very similar in composition.

island arc. A volcanic chain that rises directly from the ocean floor and is associated with a subduction zone.

isotopes. Atoms of the same chemical element that differ slightly in their mass.

kimberlite. A volcanic rock from deep in the mantle that can bear diamonds.

komatiite. An ancient, magnesium-rich magma that was the result of a very high degree of partial melting of the mantle.

lahar. A mudflow that occurs on the side of a volcano.

lapilli. Erupted fragments of lava measuring between ⁵⁄₆₄ and 2½ inches (2 and 64 millimeters) in diameter.

lava. A high-temperature, silicate liquid (occasionally carbonate) erupted from a volcano.

lava fountain. A continuous jet of lava that is the result of the uninterrupted vesiculation of rising magma.

liquid. A state of matter characterized by a random or poorly organized arrangement of atoms.

lithosphere. The roughly 60-mile-thick (100-kilometer-thick) outer layer of the earth that comprises the crust and the rigid part of the upper mantle; it rests above the asthenospheric mantle.

lithospheric plate. *See* plate

maar. A crater formed by violent phreatic explosions that occur when water and magma interact.

magma. A liquid formed by partial melting of rock that may erupt at the surface as lava.

magma chamber. An accumulation of magma in the mantle or crust.

magmatic differentiation. The chemical evolution of a magma due to fractional crystallization.

mantle. The solid layer between the crust and the outer core, composed mainly of silicon, magnesium, and oxygen.

matrix. The finer-grained, sometimes glassy material that surrounds larger crystals, which are sometimes phenocrysts.

melt. The liquid phase that results from the partial melting of the mantle or crustal rocks. In a broader sense, *melt* is frequently used as a synonym for *magma*, but volcanologists recognize magma as the liquid that moves up from depth, fills magma chambers, and sometimes erupts at the earth's surface.

microlite. A small, lath-shaped crystal.

microlitic texture. A rock texture in which microlites are the more-abundant crystal.

mid-ocean ridge. A linear chain of submarine mountains that occur where oceanic crust forms.

mixing (magma). A physical process by which two or more magmas of different compositions are mixed and form lavas of intermediate composition.

nuée ardente. French for "glowing cloud." A hot, dense pyroclastic flow erupted from a volcano.

obsidian. Black or dark-colored natural volcanic glass.

pāhoehoe. A basaltic lava flow with a smooth, ropy, or draped surface.

Peléan eruption. The violent explosion of a viscous dome that has not degassed. These eruptions are characterized by pyroclastic flows.

Pelé's hair. Thin strands of volcanic glass.

peridotite. A rock predominantly composed of the minerals olivine and pyroxene; it is the principle component of the upper mantle, whereas at greater depth the lower mantle is composed of its high-pressure equivalents.

perlitic. A texture of vitrified silica-rich rocks that is characterized by small beadlike features.

phenocryst. A large, well-formed crystal that grows as magma cools slowly in a magma chamber.

phreatic eruption. An explosive eruption of jets of steam caused when rising magma heats groundwater.

phreatic water. Water that has percolated into the ground, saturating porous and permeable rocks; groundwater.

phreatomagmatic eruption. A phreatic eruption that emits magma as well as jets of steam.

pillow lava. A rounded bulb of lava formed when the lava's surface cools rapidly upon contact with cold seawater or lake water.

pipe. *See* feeder pipe

plate. A rigid piece of the lithosphere that is composed of the crust and upper part of the mantle.

plate tectonics. A theory in which the earth's surface is composed of plates that move up to 4 inches (about 10 centimeters) per year, driven by mantle convection. Much of the earth's volcanic activity occurs at the boundaries of these plates.

Plinian eruption. A very explosive eruption caused by the sudden vesiculation of magma. These eruptions are characterized by pumice plumes and pumice deposits.

plume. (1) A mushroom-shaped cloud of pumice, lapilli, ash, and gas that rises high above a volcano following a Plinian or Peléan eruption. (2) A localized region of hot material with relatively low density that rises in the mantle. Mantle plumes are associated with hot spots.

porcellanite. A rock formed by the thermal metamorphism of a clay horizon adjacent to basalt.

porphyritic texture. A rock texture in which large, well-formed crystals are surrounded by a fine-grained matrix.

pumice. A highly vesicular lava that has a very low density.

pyroclastic flow. A dense, hot mixture of pyroclastic material and gas ejected from a volcano.

pyroclasts. Volcanic fragments—ash, lapilli, bombs—thrown out during violent eruptions. This material can form thick pyroclastic deposits.

radioactive. Relating to an unstable element that decays to form a daughter element by giving off radiation.

radioactive decay. A process in which an unstable isotope of an element changes into an isotope of another element by emitting energetic particles, for example, electrons or alpha particles.

radiogenic. Said of the isotope (daughter) produced by radioactive decay.

rhyolite. A volcanic rock rich in silicon, sodium, and potassium; it is derived from magmas that originate within the continental crust and sometimes from extreme fractional crystallization of a basaltic magma.

ropy lava. A basaltic lava with a surface texture that resembles loose coils of rope.

scoria. A coarse, vesicular pyroclastic rock that can accumulate around a vent, forming scoria cones.

seafloor spreading. The lateral movement of two oceanic plates away from each other on either side of a mid-ocean ridge. It is a major component of plate tectonics.

seismic foci. A point in the earth's crust or mantle where fracturing occurs and triggers a seismic shock.

seismic waves. Energy waves or vibrations generated by earthquakes. Geologists interpret their trajectory through the earth in order to gather information about the earth's structure.

series (magmatic or lava). A genetically associated series of volcanic rocks derived from a common magma that has experienced fractional crystallization or magma mixing or both.

sill. A sheetlike magma body that is intruded parallel—usually roughly horizontal—to surrounding rock formations.

source (magmatic). Areas of the crust or mantle that undergo partial melting and provide rhyolitic or basaltic magmas.

Strombolian eruption. An eruption following the expansion of gas bubbles in a feeder pipe, which forces bubble-rich magma to the surface.

subduction. The downward movement of a lithospheric plate into the asthenosphere. It is a major component of plate tectonics.

surge. A gas-rich pyroclastic flow.

texture. The arrangement of particles or crystals in a rock.

tremor. A seismic vibration of the earth caused by the movement of magma.

tube. A long, narrow conduit that channels lava downslope. Low-viscosity basaltic eruptions commonly produce tubes both underwater and on dry land.

tuff. A rock deposit composed of ash.

tuff ring. A ring of pyroclastic material surrounding a maar crater.

tunnel. A hollow conduit that remains after molten lava has drained out of a lava tube.

vent. An opening at the earth's surface from which magma is erupted.

vesiculation. The separation of gas bubbles from magma through decompression.

volcanic cone. A conical structure composed of lava and pyroclastic deposits.

volcanic ejecta. Fragments of lava and basement rock that are ejected by a volcano.

wedge (mantle). A region of relatively hot mantle above a subduction zone in which partial melting occurs as a plate that is being subducted loses its water.

xenolith. A rock that is different than the magma that carries it up from depth; from the Greek *xeno* for "foreign" and *lithos* for "rock."

INDEX

95